AN A~Z OF
GEMS
AND
JEWELRY

AN A~Z OF GEMS AND JEWELRY

Bill Robins

Arco Publishing, Inc.
New York

Published by Arco Publishing, Inc.
219 Park Avenue South, New York, N.Y. 10003

© Bill Robins 1982

Library of Congress Cataloging in Publication Data

Robins, Bill.
  An A–Z of gems and jewelry.
  1. Jewelry—Dictionaries. 2. Precious stones—
  Dictionaries. I. Title. II. An A Z of gems and
  jewelry.
  TS722.R6   739.27'03'21   81–19084
  ISBN 0–668–05465–4   AACR2

Printed in Great Britain

INTRODUCTION

Most people can recognise a few well known gems but the techniques and terminology of the jeweler's craft usually remain a mystery. The purchase of jewelry – perhaps to mark some momentous occasion such as a birthday or a wedding – often depends solely on aesthetic appeal, even if the item is bought as an investment. Few would enter into the similarly major purchase of, say, a car or television, without consulting some source of reference or taking advice, but such care and forethought are not always given to the choice of a ring or a bracelet. Reliance on the integrity and goodwill of the jeweler is seldom misplaced but a greater knowledge and understanding of any acquisition can only add to its interest.

Finding information on jewelry is not easy. Many books have been written, but the field is so varied that each title tends to specialise – some deal with historical aspects, or craftsmen in a particular discipline – and many are aimed at the connoisseur or the already knowledgeable.

An A–Z of Gems and Jewelry is a simple, non-technical guide, providing a summary of all the principal precious and semi-precious gems and materials used in a craft that dates back to man's earliest history. In addition, there are concise explanations of the terminology in common use and descriptions of the styles and fashions that are constantly changing and evolving in the esoteric world of jewelry.

It is hoped that reading this book will enable you to appreciate more fully the skill and imagination needed to create a piece of jewelry, and give you some idea of the enormous variety of natural riches to be found in the earth.

Agate

One of the most prolific of natural stones, found in a wide variety of colours, ranging from black to white, with variations of yellow, grey, red and brown. Flecks and striations of contrasting colours give it an interesting character. Several methods exist for dyeing agate to achieve different colour effects and to emphasise the contrasting colours of the veinings. White agate was employed in much Victorian jewellery especially as a background material in brooches with turquoises or other semi-precious stones as overlay sprays or sprigs.

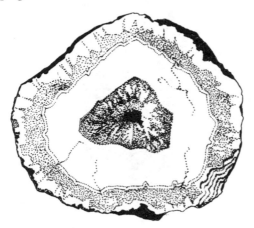

(*Above*) Agate in its natural state. (*Below*) The veins of contrasting colour can be emphasised by polishing and dyeing

Aiglets

Also called agulets or aglets. These are little metal tags or sheaths for the ends of ribbons, mainly worn in the sixteenth and seventeenth centuries.

Aigrette

Not to be confused with the above. A diamond head ornament worn to one side of the hair like a plume, from which its name is derived.

A late eighteenth-century diamond and silver aigrette. The 'stalks' are designed to quiver with every movement of the wearer

Alexandrite

A unique optical feature characterises this stone. In daylight it appears green, or a greenish-brown, but under artificial (yellow) light it shows a distinct reddish colour. Originally found in Russia, it was named after Tsar Alexander II and became favoured by the Court. Later, it was discovered also in Sri Lanka. The colour in the stone is due to the presence of chromium (a metal which also gives the green in emeralds and the red in rubies) and the balance between green and red is so evenly matched in this stone that the greater proportion of red found in artificial light is sufficient to tip the scale.

It is one of the large family of chrysoberyls. Genuine alexandrites are rare, but they are made synthetically, and the majority offered as real are usually the man-made variety.

Alloys
See Gold

Amber
A substance of great antiquity, amber is the fossilised resin of prehistoric conifer trees. It is unlike any other semi-precious material used in jewellery, being very light in weight and never really cold to the touch. It is found in a wide range of colours, from white to dark red and even black. Through the ages different colours have been favoured with changing uses and fashions.

The shores of the Baltic provide the golden yellow to orange type, but some of the rarest ambers originate in Sicily, Rumania and Burma. Nearly all varieties are found in clear and cloudy types, and some have small inclusions of fragments of leaves or tiny pieces of bark, locked in when the amber was in its liquid stage. Specimens with entrapped midges, flies and other insects are rare and sought by collectors and museums.

Amber is mainly used in jewellery for beads, but some specimens are carved for pendants. Such rows of beads are common in Greek and Arab lands as prayer necklaces; their lightness enables them to be carried easily and played through the fingers.

In early days magic powers were attributed to the material. An amulet of amber was believed to protect the wearer against evil, and to work as a cure for many ills. It was ground into a powder and used as a medicine in the sixteenth century, and it was sometimes burnt for its aroma or as a fumigant.

Named *electron* by the Greeks, amber has the faculty of attracting tiny particles of paper or hairs to cling to it after being rubbed on a sleeve or fabric. However, this characteristic of having static electricity is by no means conclusive, as many other materials, including some plastics, display the same feature. But if it does not pick up particles at all, it can usually be dismissed as not being genuine.

Smaller and crude pieces of amber can be fused together into what is called pressed amber, from which carvings and larger items can be made.

Amethyst
This stone is a variety of quartz, one of the most common of minerals, and thus would not normally rank very highly in the hierarchy of gems. But because of its antiquity and its beautiful violet or mauve colour, the amethyst has attained an eminent

position among gemstones, and prices have risen steeply over the years. Generally the deeper the colour the more costly and highly prized it has become. Possibly some of this importance has arisen from the magnificent suites of amethyst jewellery made for the Russian royal families in the eighteenth and nineteenth centuries when Russia had first claim on the finest specimens mined in the Ural mountains. It gained prestige also by its employment in bishops' rings, and in finely carved Renaissance signet rings and seals.

The name of the stone derives from a Greek word meaning 'not drunken', which gave rise to the belief that the wearing of the stone gave immunity to the after effects of over-indulgence.

This gold mounted amethyst and pearl necklace and pendant cross is late Victorian but the design is reminiscent of an earlier Gothic style

Aquamarine

No gem has a more descriptive name than the aquamarine, suggestive of the clear bluish green of the waters in a tropical cove. It is a member of the beryl family – the finest of which is the emerald.

It is not a brilliant stone, having comparatively low refractivity, but depends on its size and purity of colour for effect. Also, it is usually free of flaws or inclusions so that a large plain surface is available, and this is best displayed by the minimum of cutting. The usual presentation is a square or rectangular stone, step cut – a flat top surface with slight canted or cut steps at the sides only.

At one time the bluish-green aquamarine was the most favoured, but today the purer and clearer blue is preferred; the richer the blue the more it is valued.

Main supplies come from Brazil, the Ural mountains, Sri Lanka, India, South Africa and several of the United States. As aquamarines are available in comparative abundance they are often employed in a suite; several mounted as a bracelet, a larger number for a necklace, two stones in drop form for a pair of ear rings, and a selected specimen for a ring.

Aqua Regia

For testing 18-carat and finer standards of gold, and platinum, a special combination of acids is required, known as aqua regia. Composed of three parts of hydrochloric acid to one part of nitric acid by volume, diluted with water, this mixture dissolves the metal.

Art Nouveau

One of the most imaginative innovations in the history of design was the development of the art nouveau movement. Emerging in the last quarter of the nineteenth century, it brought together dreamers and idealists seeking a world of symbolic mysticism and those who saw the machine age as providing the means of spreading art and beauty through all sectors of society.

Art nouveau encompassed a style of free-flowing rhythmic patterns often based on natural forms of flowers and fernery, and swirling abstractions, giving an ornamental line to every article. It inspired furniture, silver, pottery, glass, paintings and posters, and architecture. It was a movement which originated mainly in England and spread throughout the Continent and America.

In jewellery, the style broke with many traditions and created

11

Art nouveau brooches, set with
diamonds, pearls and translucent
enamel. The peacock motif and the
flowing design of the flowers are both
typical of the style

12

new forms and novel treatments of old materials, often being inspired by Oriental art. In England the firm of Liberty produced a wide range of silver and jewellery under their brand name of Cymric, combining machine made and hand crafted pieces in association with a Birmingham firm, W. H. Haseler. The silver jewellery embraced buckles, pendants, brooches, bracelets, hair ornaments, ear rings and rings featuring much enamelling, and items inlaid with turquoise, opals, pearls and amethysts.

Probably the most influential jeweller associated with the movement was René Lalique of Paris, whose spectacular displays at the Paris Centennial Exhibition of 1900 aroused enormous interest. His designs, in gold, precious gems, enamelled work and particularly plain and coloured glass, set new fashions. Another French firm, the house of Vever, run jointly by the brothers Paul and Henri, was equally industrious in manufacturing art nouveau jewellery of a high standard. Henri was the author in 1908 of *La Bijouterie Française au XIX Siècle*, the recognised work on French nineteenth-century jewellery.

In America, Louis Comfort Tiffany, the son of America's most fashionable and expensive jeweller, transformed and adapted art nouveau to meet the demands of his wealthy clients. He perfected a form of iridescent glass, used almost entirely in decorative domestic products.

Although the movement was halted by World War I, it continued to influence designers in almost every field for many years, and its products have recently enjoyed a strong revival of interest.

Assay

Neither gold nor silver are suitable for making into jewellery in the pure state. Both are too soft and require a small percentage of some other metal to provide the hardness for fabricating. Consequently, it is necessary to establish the purity of the alloy to ascertain its percentage of pure gold or silver. The method of carrying this out is called the assay, undertaken at assay offices legally established for the purpose. Every article of gold or silver that is manufactured is subject to such tests before qualifying for its appropriate hall-mark. A tiny scraping of the metal is taken from the finished article, in some place where it will not do any damage, before it receives its final polishing. Only if it conforms to the standards laid down will it receive its stamps indelibly impressed into the metal.

For silver, the standard must be at least 925 parts per 1,000 pure

13

silver (92.5 per cent), but for gold there are currently four accepted grades – 9, 14, 18 and 22 carats, these numbers representing the number of parts out of 24 of pure gold.

At one time there were a large number of assay offices throughout Britain. Today, there are only four, London, Birmingham, Sheffield and Edinburgh, each of which has a symbol or stamp to indicate the particular office at which the article was tested. (*See also* Hall-marks)

Aventurine
One of the many varieties of quartz, distinguished by flashing specks of mica embodied in its structure. Mainly found in shades of red, yellow and brown, it is very similar to aventurine feldspar which has golden specks. The name aventurine is more commonly given, though incorrectly, to a glass melt in which there are crystals of copper. Because of its gilt specks, the material is also frequently described as goldstone.

Baguette
While the central feature of a ring is normally a single diamond, a number of diamonds, or a coloured gem of some kind, an interesting and rich effect is frequently given by having additional narrow, rectangular or baton-cut diamonds on the shoulders. There are often a series of these flanking the main jewel, graduated in size, for which the term baguette is applied.

Baton
This is a type of cutting, usually applied to diamonds, in narrow, rectangular strip form.

Beryl
There are several members of the beryl family of gems, the choicest of which are the emerald and aquamarine. The green variety is known as the beryl, the golden yellow gem as heliodor, while the pink or rose coloured specimen is the morganite.

Bezel
The flat top, or table, of a signet ring. In making a ring in primitive days from a strip of metal, the jeweller would hammer out one part to flatten it and then, if desired, punch this bezel with symbols or an inscription, making it suitable for impressing on wax.

Birthstones

Myth and superstition have always been part of the ancient lore surrounding gems. Each known stone had its attributed powers, and a relation was found between them and astronomical periods. There was a strong belief that for each month there was an accredited gem, and that those born in the month, or the relative zodiacal period, would acquire the special benefits of that gem if they wore it. Hence the origin of the birthstone.

But tradition, being varied, resulted in different stones being selected in separate countries as appropriate. At one time, the chosen lists for Roman, Arabic, Jewish, Polish, Russian and Italian birthstones had little unanimity. One of the principal reasons for this variation was because, in ancient times, stones were judged and named largely by their colour, and colour became the main factor in picking a stone appropriate for a given month. Moreover, in the eighteenth century a practice grew up of selecting a second, or alternative stone. This provided the opportunity of offering a less expensive gem in many instances.

Committees representing the retail interests in Britain and America reached agreement some fifty years ago and have since accepted the official stones for each month as listed below. The alternatives for March and August (bloodstone and sardonyx), although not of the appropriate colour, have been included because of strong traditions linking them to these particular months.

Month	Colour	Official Stone	Alternative
January	Dark red	Garnet	—
February	Purple	Amethyst	—
March	Pale blue	Aquamarine	Bloodstone
April	White (clear)	Diamond	Rock crystal
May	Bright green	Emerald	Chrysoprase
June	Cream	Pearl	Moonstone
July	Red	Ruby	Cornelian
August	Pale green	Peridot	Sardonyx
September	Deep blue	Sapphire	Lapis lazuli
October	Variegated	Opal	—
November	Yellow	Topaz	—
December	Sky blue	Turquoise	—

Bishop's Ring

A handsome and important ring, given on conferring office on a bishop, together with his pastoral staff. Such episcopal rings date back many centuries; a document records one in 633. These rings were generally of gold set with a large single stone, a sapphire, ruby or amethyst, and often with chasing or engraving on the mount. They were invariably large as they were worn over the glove.

Bishops' rings were endowed with mystical significance. It is believed that originally they were a symbol of authority, given by the reigning monarch and returned to him on the wearer's death. They are very uncommon in private collections as most have been preserved in the cathedrals where they have been found.

Bloodstone
A dark-green stone with speckles of red, much used for men's signet rings. The stone, alternatively called blood jasper, mineralogically is chalcedony, a member of the quartz species. (*See also* Chalcedony; Quartz)

Blue John
A form of fluorspar found mainly in Derbyshire. Rich blue with a slightly speckled appearance, Blue John is not unlike lapis lazuli, but is a much softer material. Its main use in jewellery is for men's signet rings, but many larger pieces are quarried and carved into urns and vases. It is known also as fluorite, the usual term for other coloured varieties.

Bolt Ring
See Fastenings

Box Snap
See Fastenings

Brilliant
Another term for a diamond which has been cut into 58 facets, a system mathematically worked out to achieve the maximum brilliance of the stone. (*See also* Cutting)

Buckles
Among the earliest buckles are medieval specimens, beautifully decorative, but these are considered to have formed part of the harness or trappings for horses.

For shoes they came into favour in the seventeenth century and then went out of fashion again until the early part of the eighteenth, when they blossomed out into large and ornate types.

A silver and gilt buckle in the art nouveau style, set with semi-precious stones

A great variety of materials and skilled workmanship was expended on them. The richest types encompassed diamonds set in silver, sometimes even gold, and for those who could not afford such, the use of paste gems, cut steel and other substitutes were employed to give a sparkling effect. Other styles were made in pewter, enamel, mother of pearl, jet and pinchbeck, and the famous Wedgwood factory produced special cameos to adorn them.

Buckles designed for the waist followed this fashion closely, though they were smaller. Shoe buckles can be distinguished by their greater curvature, sometimes almost semicircular.

Although they have largely gone out of fashion for shoes, buckles have continued down to the present day for Court dress and are worn by bishops, judges and as part of full Highland dress. Small-size fancy buckles are popular as an ornament for neckwear.

Cabochon

Before the art of cutting facets upon hard precious gems was known, the jeweller was content to give a polish to the natural material without greatly altering its shape. Most such gems were found as rounded, water-worn objects and, when polished to produce a domed effect, established the style known as cabochon. The degree of curvature can vary from the shallow curve used for opals and small turquoises to the steeply arched, almost pointed, shape used for 'star' sapphires and rubies.

The underside of a cabochon gem is usually polished flat; but in very dark stones, such as a garnet, the underside is sometimes

G & J b

hollowed out to make it appear brighter. The name 'carbuncle' (glowing coal) was given to such stones, and this term is often used to describe a cabochon-cut gem of any variety.

Cairngorm
The name given to the yellowish-brown variety of smoky quartz, examples of which are found in Scotland and used in much Celtic jewellery. The cairngorm is often wrongly called Scottish topaz. (*See also* Celtic jewellery)

Calibre
A form of cutting a gem to a particular shape to fit a design. In most jewellery the stones are bought or cut in their standard form and then set within the design envisaged. In some cases, however, it is desired to fit the stones exactly to the pattern, as in a jigsaw, so the gem is cut specially. Many modern pieces of jewellery call for such particular outlines, in which the lapidary has to work strictly to the measurements laid down by the designer or artist.

Cameo
The cameo, a form of sculpture in relief, involves fine hand-carving to cut away the top surface of a stone or shell, revealing darker shades below. The finest and earliest cameos, some dating from the Sumerian period, were carved in hard stones and precious gems – agate, onyx, jasper, amethyst, emerald, malachite – and worked with exquisite skill. The carver would take advantage, for instance, of the different layers of colour in an onyx stone to give tone and depth to a portrait head or figure.

A nineteenth-century shell cameo, set with amazonite, coral and mother of pearl

For shell cameos, special shells which provide layers of different colours are needed in order to provide contrast; among these are the Queen's Conch, with a pinky under-layer; the Bull's Mouth, with a red base; and the Black Helmet, a white shell with dark brown for the under-layer. Italy became the great centre for shell cameo work and many fine specimens have been produced. Unfortunately, shell scratches and fractures easily, and damaged ones should be avoided, as should any that have not been carved with fine detail and depth.

Throughout the ages cameos have been used for rings, bracelets and pendants, and larger samples for decorating cabinets, boxes and other furniture. Many today are mass produced, usually of classical heads or figures multiplied in thousands, and some so-called cameos are in fact stamped or pressed in plastic or other compositions.

Lesser valued cameos are also made from the coloured lava of Pompeii in brown, cream and muddy greens.

Carat

The term 'carat' is used in jewellery for two quite different purposes. In the case of gold it defines the purity of the metal, 24 carats being pure gold. As pure gold is too soft for fabricating into jewellery it is alloyed with other metals, the legal standards being 22, 18, 14 and 9 carats, the numbers referring to the amount of pure gold per 24 parts. In its other sense, carat is used to define the weight of diamonds and other precious stones, being one-fifth of a gram (200 milligrams). This metric definition of the weight of gems became adopted as standard in Britain in 1914. Previously it was expressed in the same term as for gold and silver – troy ounces.

For pearls a smaller unit is employed, namely the pearl grain, which is one-fourth of a carat (50 milligrams).

The system of weights obtaining in various parts of the ancient world for measuring gems was based upon the seeds of plants which were nearly uniform in size and weight. In the countries bordering the Mediterranean, the locust tree, *Ceratonia siliqua*, produces seeds that have an average weight nearly equal to the carat, and was probably the origin of this term. (*See also* Gold; Hall-marks)

Castellani, Fortunato

Some of the choicest jewellery of the nineteenth century was made with the object of reviving the styles of the ancient world. The exquisite filigree and granulation work in Etruscan, Greek and

19

Roman pieces were admired, but the techniques were unknown. In Rome, Pio Fortunato Castellani (1793–1865) devoted himself for many years to a close study of this early work, achieving results which, if not as fine as the originals, were quite remarkable. He was a perfectionist – who incidentally found that women were better fitted than male goldsmiths to undertake the delicate work involved – and his ideals were carried on by his two sons, Augusto and Alessandro. Augusto improved on his father's virtuosity. He also made a beautiful collection of Italian and other peasant jewellery now housed in the Victoria and Albert Museum, in London. One of the results of Augusto's efforts was the rediscovery of making granulation work and affixing the tiny droplets in lines and patterns.

A gold bangle by Castellani, set with carved agate

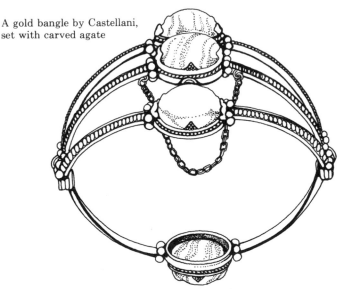

Cat's Eye

A few gems possess a peculiar optical effect – a line of light that seems to run across the stone as it is turned this way and that. Because it gives the illusion of the gleam of an animal's eye, the effect is known as 'cat's eye'. The name, strictly speaking, should be applied only to the translucent honey-coloured stone chrysoberyl, which shows this strange streak of light; but the same effect is found in varieties of quartz and in the sapphire. The effect in the yellow-brown quartz is also described as tiger's eye, and in the grey-blue quartz as falcon's eye.

Cellini, Benvenuto

One of the most celebrated names in the world of the art of jewellery was Benvenuto Cellini (1500–71), regarded as the greatest jeweller goldsmith of the Renaissance. The ateliers of goldsmiths, where Cellini began his career, were recognised as unrivalled centres for learning the art of fine drawing. Many who served their apprenticeships at the craft devoted themselves to painting and sculpture later, providing the world with master-pieces. Cellini remained a goldsmith throughout his life, devoting himself to studying the classical Roman period and writing extensively on his work and describing pieces of jewellery he had made. Yet, strangely, little material evidence of his work survives. A necklace in the Desmond collection in New York is, however, attributed to him, and his own records tell of special jewels made by him for Pope Clement II and of a ring made for Pope Paul III.

Cellini's work was distinguished by rich enamelling, pearls and table-cut gems, exquisitely wrought figures and scenes that are works of art in themselves.

Celtic Jewellery

Celtic brooches, although generally identified with Scotland, were really a jewellery style which extended to Ireland, Wales and Brittany – in fact wherever the Celts established themselves.

The earliest specimen is the Hunterston brooch, found on an Ayrshire hillside, which dates from AD 700. It is of silver, and a fine example of delicate silversmith work. Many Celtic brooches are of a similar pattern – circular with a long, hinged, vertical pin. Later

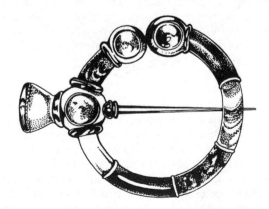

Celtic brooch set with a cairngorm

21

Celtic jewellery. Traditional designs for brooches, rings and scarf pins

copies featured the thistle, often with a cairngorm or Scottish pebble inset, the claymore or the dirk. Others were based on the St Andrew's Cross (diagonal) and the Iona Cross, with four equal square ends. These motifs are not confined to brooches, but are seen as pendants, and tie and scarf pins. Although the earliest specimens were produced in bronze or silver, gold was occasionally employed, and in Victorian Celtic jewellery much use was made of traditional Scottish stones such as cairngorm and amethyst, or pearls from Scottish rivers.

Chain

The simple loop-in-loop chain was known some four thousand years ago and, with variations in design, has remained in use until the present day. One of its attractions as a personal adornment is its flexibility, altering with every movement of the wearer.

The various designs of chain have their trade names. *Trace*, the simplest, is of oval, equal sized links; *Belcher* has equal sized links of rather wider material; *Alma* is also broad, with the surface of each link ribbed; *Fetter* has long links, often interspersed with smaller links; and in the *Curb* design the links are given a twist causing them to lie down flatter against each other, almost forming a band. A woven band is the *Milanese* with very tiny close links, produced in various widths and often in mixed colours of gold, giving a rich effect. The *Brazilian* chain, made by special machinery, is the most flexible of all, being of rope or snake-like form. There are, of course, a multitude of fancy patterns with variations of links, some with several links meshed together in parallel. The popular *Prince of Wales* or rope chain gives the appearance of two thick strands woven into one.

Large gold chains worn round the neck have served various purposes throughout the ages. The term 'guard chain' refers to a tradition that goes back to medieval times, when the lady of the castle or manor safeguarded her keys by attaching them to the chain. Usually the chain ended in a special holder, or châtelaine, from which not only her keys, but small useful or toilet articles such as scissors and needle cases were suspended. In other periods the chain held a watch on a swivel, or was clipped on to a muff. (*See also* Necklace)

Victorian gold Albert chains

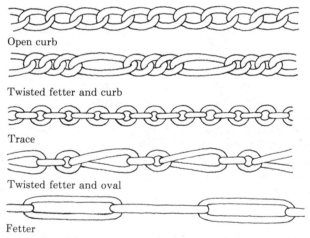

Open curb

Twisted fetter and curb

Trace

Twisted fetter and oval

Fetter

Chalcedony

A mineral group belonging to the quartz species, chalcedony is found in a variety of colours, sometimes plain, but more usually with distinctive bandings and striations. The dark-green chalcedony with spots of red is popularly described as bloodstone. The same family of stones provides sard, in a brownish red colour, and sardonyx, which has a brownish red layer (sard) and a second layer banded in black, grey, white or brown, the typical patterning of onyx.

Charms

Miniature items, especially if carried out in accurate detail, are of universal appeal. In jewellery, known as charms, they add novelty and movement to a bracelet, and provide an opportunity for the goldsmith to exercise his art and skill in producing tiny replicas.

Charms can be more than mere novelties; they frequently serve as some kind of talisman, or have a symbolic meaning, such as the so-called 'lucky' pig or old boot, or the St Christopher emblem carried as a safeguard for the traveller. The range of charms is enormous. Animals rank high – horses, dogs, cats, owls. The sporting interest of a wearer can be shown in hunting horns, foxes, guns, footballs or hockey sticks. Motor cars, radios, and other contemporary objects are featured, while hearts, flowers, arrows, crosses and names symbolise affection.

Gold or silver charms can be collected on a bracelet for symbolic or sentimental reasons, or simply because of the fascination of their exquisite miniature detail

Chasing

Chasing is a technique for decorating the plain surface of silver and gold which, while seen at its best in larger silverware, is used in jewellery in a more subdued style. It is performed by virtually coaxing the metal into the right places by delicate use of punches and a hammer. This does not remove the metal, as in engraving, but tends to make it rise into slight ridges. Small repeat patterns are built up in this way, or detail given to an outline of, say, a bird or fish, to indicate plumage or scales (*See also* Engraving)

Chenier

The fine hollow tubing known as chenier provides a means of making the functional parts of jewellery – hinges, safety catches, joints, etc – light, strong and unobtrusive. Hollow tubes are more difficult to bend than solid metal but, if necessary, they can be reinforced by the insertion of a rod. This method allows a considerable saving in gold. Most jewellery craftsmen make their own chenier but it can be obtained from bullion dealers, machine made, in varying diameters and in round, square or other profiles.

Chrysoberyl

The wide range of stones, such as emerald and aquamarine, belonging to the beryl family vary in degrees of hardness. The hardest is the chrysoberyl, ranking as the third hardest gem variety. Although often seen as a clear yellow or golden stone, the most favoured variety is that which displays the feature known as 'cat's eye', in which a streak of light appears to move across the translucent honey-coloured or greenish yellow surface as the gem is turned in direction. The movement is more silky and effective than in the commoner quartz cat's eye. In fact chrysoberyl is the only gem with this characteristic to which the term cat's eye may be applied on its own, without the additional designation of the name of the stone. It is always cut cabochon to exhibit this attractive feature.

Cire Perdue (Lost Wax Process)

This is a very ancient method of casting a piece of jewellery or small sculptured item which will eventually be seen from all angles 'in the round'. It was used in Egypt in the XII dynasty, and for the production of fine enamelled jewels of the Renaissance period.

The design is first modelled in detail in hard wax, then packed round with clay. The wax is melted away through air passages, and replaced with molten metal. When set, the clay is broken away. Although a very faithful copy of the original is produced, the process is of limited use in commercial work, as only one object can be made unless a further wax model is prepared for every fresh casting. The method is still occasionally employed for individual items of artistic merit by designers.

Citrine

Of the very large family of quartz, citrine is the yellow variety. The name is an adaptation of the French for lemon, although the colours range from palest yellow to golden brown. It is often wrongly described as topaz, but the latter stone is rare and more costly, and to prevent confusion is almost always described as a Brazilian topaz. The use of the term topaz for citrine has been ruled an illegal description.

Coral

This material is gathered from the seabed rocks in the warm waters of the Mediterranean and around Japan, and is formed from the skeletal remains of coral polyp colonies. In its natural state it grows irregularly, in twig-like shapes which in earlier days were simply drilled and threaded to be worn as necklaces and bracelets. It can be polished and carved to make round beads, carved into cameos or into stylised shapes for the centrepieces of brooches or rings. The craftsmen who specialise in this work are nearly all centred in Torre del Graco near Naples.

Italian coral ranges in colour from white, through pink to reds of deepening hue, and of these the deepest red is the most prized. Most highly valued of all, however, is the delicate shell or flesh pink of Japanese coral with a rose sheen almost like a pink pearl.

A belief was long held that coral had some protective quality, which made it popular as a traditional gift for children. It featured in beautiful Georgian rattles for babies, complete with a whistle and bells, a piece of coral being employed as the teething 'ring'.

Ornamental comb with polished coral beads

Cornelian

The name given to the reddish variety of the numerous chalcedony family of stones. It is a favourite material for beads, and also for signet and seal rings as it lends itself well to intaglio engraving. Colours vary from a yellowish red to brownish red, and because bright red is popular, but somewhat rare, dyeing is often resorted to.

26

Crystal

A type of colourless quartz, rock crystal is used in necklaces, either on its own or interspersed with coloured stones. At first glance it may not appear very different from faceted glass, but there is a sharpness of edge in the cutting and a keen flash of light in the natural material. It is found in many parts of the world, the larger pieces coming from Brazil.

When tinged with brown it is better known as the cairngorm, and as citrine when clear yellow, while the purple variety is the familiar amethyst. (*See also* Quartz)

Cutting

Until methods of cutting precious stones were developed, the ancient jeweller was content to give a polish to the natural material without substantially altering its shape. When techniques were discovered for cutting into the stone, the art of shaping and producing facets on the surface greatly enhanced the brilliance and reflective qualities. A number of styles were developed to emphasise these qualities. At first, facets were cut on the dome. Later, other styles developed, depending partly on the original shape of the gem, its nature and colour, and partly on the type of setting for which it was intended.

In its most skilled application, cutting is practised on diamonds by a diamond polisher; a lapidarist generally devotes himself to coloured stones and lesser gems.

The best known styles of cutting are:

Brilliant: a style which has been mathematically devised to produce the greatest brilliance. It has 58 facets, of which 33 are above the girdle (the widest part of the gem which is held in the setting) and 25 below.

Rose cut: an older style, dating from Elizabethan times, in which all the facets are above the girdle, and the bottom is flat. The facets are all triangular in shape. This style is useful for smaller stones and cuts economically from the rough.

Emerald cut: also known as trap cut. This is used mainly for square or rectangular stones, such as emeralds and aquamarines. There are no top facets, the upper surface being polished smooth, but canted or step cut at the sides.

There are also variations and combinations of cutting styles. A type with a brilliant cut front and step-cut back is known as a mixed cut. For pendant ear rings, a drop-shape cut, known as the briolette, shows the principle of the rose cut applied right round the whole surface of the stone. Faceting a round or elliptical stone

Cutting styles for precious stones

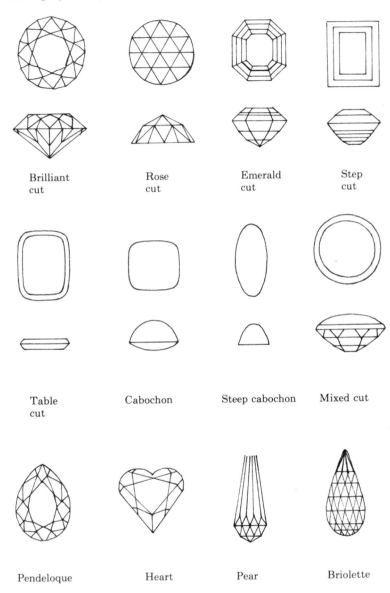

Brilliant
cut

Rose
cut

Emerald
cut

Step
cut

Table
cut

Cabochon

Steep cabochon

Mixed cut

Pendeloque

Heart

Pear

Briolette

by square or kite-shaped facets is called a bead cut. (*See also* Baguette; Baton; Calibre)

Damascening
In Eastern and Mediterranean countries during the Middle Ages a fine art was practised of inlaying gold or silver on some inferior metal, generally steel in early examples. Rings, breastplates and armour were embellished in this manner, employing fine detailed work. The process was extended in later years to large articles such as urns, salvers and ecclesiastical dishes, but the workmanship tended to be poorer.

Decade Ring
A type of ring which took the place of a rosary. The earliest known is believed to date from the fourteenth century. Decade rings had ten projections and a bezel or larger knob. Each projection represented an Ave and the bezel the Paternoster.

Diadem
See Tiara

Diamond
Of all jewels, the diamond is supreme, worthy of the name precious stone. It qualifies for all the virtues implied in that term – brilliance, hardness, rarity, antiquity and permanence. It is the hardest of all gems (10 on Mohs' scale) and will scratch all gems of a lesser hardness. The diamond's origins date back millions of years to when it was formed in the Earth almost entirely from a simple element, carbon.

Every diamond, large or small, has the same crystalline structure. In particular, the diamond has an exceptionally high refractive index, accounting for the brilliance it displays in its setting. However, this is diminished or enhanced by the manner in which it is cut.

The most valuable diamonds, apart from their size, are the very pure and lustrous white stones, said to be of 'first water'. But there are many colours and tones, ranging from blue-white, through pink, yellow and mauve. A really deep coloured stone of pure tint is highly prized. A yellowish tinge to a 'white' stone is however detrimental, and tiny inclusions – black spots or other flaws – detract substantially from a diamond's value.

Some unusual cutting styles for diamonds

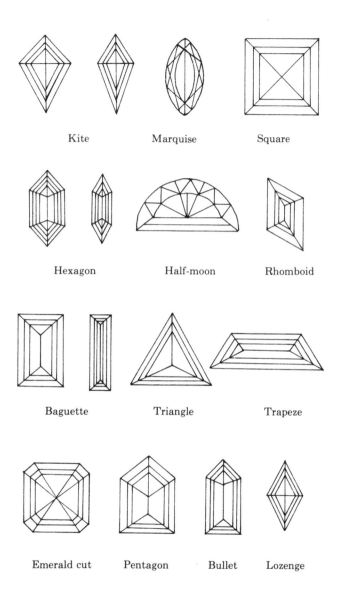

Kite   Marquise   Square

Hexagon   Half-moon   Rhomboid

Baguette   Triangle   Trapeze

Emerald cut   Pentagon   Bullet   Lozenge

Doublet

One of the devices used to make a diamond or other gem seem larger and better is to create a composite stone. This is achieved by cementing two stones together. If a pale stone has a rich-coloured glass base it not only makes a large stone out of a small one, but improves the colour. The combined stone is known as a doublet.

One practice is to back a thin diamond with a crystal or glass base, or 'double up' a ruby with a coloured glass background. Sometimes a third layer is added providing a triplet stone. The intention is not always fraudulent. The system is sometimes used to provide a harder wearing surface, such as a top layer of crystal to protect a softer opal. In fact opal is frequently used in doublet form as beautifully coloured varieties are often available only in thin seams, and some of the background matrix is included, or some backing material added to enable stones to be mounted successfully. Turquoise is also frequently cut with part of its own matrix attached.

Ear Ring Fittings

To hold an ear ring firmly and correctly in place on the ear requires different devices depending on whether the ears are pierced or not. For unpierced ears the usual means are clips or screws, which sometimes present problems for those with thin or short lobes.

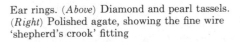

Ear rings. (*Above*) Diamond and pearl tassels. (*Right*) Polished agate, showing the fine wire 'shepherd's crook' fitting

The safest devices are provided for pierced ears. If newly pierced, a fine silver or gold circular ear-ring should be worn for some time to prevent the hole closing. They are known as 'sleepers'.

Then wire fittings can be used for drop or suspended ear rings. These are fine but hard gold or silver wires shaped like a shepherd's crook, the longish stem behind the ear helping to counterbalance the weight of the ear ring. For stud ear rings, where the pearl or gem lies flat on the lobe, it is attached to a fine straight wire passing through the lobe. This is held in place either by a small springy scroll, known as a butterfly fitting which is slid along until it grips tightly, or the wire is threaded and a threaded disc screwed on, rather like a nut and bolt.

Emerald

The rich velvety green emerald, distinct from any other green stone, is a fascinating gem, the choicest of the beryl family of stones. Most larger sizes contain slight faults or flaws, and the stone is brittle and liable to fracture. Accordingly, good sized perfect stones are extremely rare, which accounts for their costliness. A fine emerald is invariably more expensive than a similarly sized diamond.

Russian emeralds from the Ural mountains have a yellowish green hue. Lighter green specimens are found in Brazil, South Africa and Australia. The gem does not have the requisite fire or brilliance to be faceted in 'brilliant' form like a diamond; instead it is generally either en cabochon or in a rectangular or 'step cut' which has become known as 'emerald cut'. The emerald was much used in ecclesiastical and early Oriental jewellery.

Enamel

Precious and other gems have always been regarded as the keynote of fine jewellery; yet some of the richest and most colourful effects have been achieved by enamel work. It reached its highest form during the Renaissance, a period unsurpassed for magnificence and elaboration in adornment among the courts of Europe and a rich bourgeoisie in all countries. It was the age of the artist and craftsman, who created compositions in enamel on gold richly embellished by pearls and gems.

Enamel is a vitreous glaze fused to its base by heat. In a molten state glass absorbs traces of metal and other chemicals which give it colour, producing both clear and opaque enamels in a wide spectrum of shades. Different techniques are adopted to apply

Black enamel pendant with forget-me-nots inlaid in gold

these colours to ornament the jewelled object. The five principal
ones are:

Champlevé: In this process the metal groundwork is removed by
chasing, leaving a recessed design with walls, between which the
enamel is run and fired.

Basse-taille: A design is carved at the bottom of a sunken space
and a transparent enamel covers it, through which the design
shows. Sometimes detailed engraving, or in modern types, engine-
turning, is worked in the recess which sparkles through the glass-
like enamel.

Cloisonné: In this method fine wires are fixed to the metal,
determining the limits to which the enamel must keep. A single
colour of enamel is set in each section. This type of enamelling is
found in Chinese and Eastern jewellery, but mostly in larger
decorative items.

Plique-à-jour: ('Open to daylight'). A remarkably fragile stained-
glass effect is obtained by this method, using transparent enamels,
but without any supporting wires. This seemingly impossible
process is achieved by having the different colours separated by
fine wires, laid on a temporary ground, until fired. After firing the
enamel springs off the ground free of the retaining wires.

Painted enamels: This is the traditional form of painting the design
in glazes on the surface, taking care the colours do not mix.
Sometimes additional colours and later firings are given to enrich
the picture. The well known Limoge enamel paintings employ this
process.

Engraving

The decorating of plain gold and silver jewellery with incised linear designs or patterns. It is distinct from carving, in which the metal is cut to varying depths to form a raised pattern. The process was used on Georgian lockets and pendants, but more widely employed on Victorian silver items – bangles, vesta match cases, cigarette cases and fancy pendants. Engraving is used for inscriptions on the insides of wedding rings, on memorial jewellery and for monograms and inscriptions on presentation items.

An unusual mode of engraving is known as 'bright cut' in which the metal is skimmed by bevel cuttings. It provides a jewel-like faceted sparkle to the surface.

Eternity Ring

A narrow ring, normally of platinum, containing as many stones as can be mounted on its circumference. The gems are usually diamonds, rubies or sapphires, often set alternately. Other styles are twin or triple circlets, with a row of the same kind of stones on each circle. Traditionally, an eternity ring is given to a wife on an anniversary, birthday or special occasion.

Fabergé, Peter Carl

Peter Carl Fabergé (1846–1920) was the designer and maker of some of the most exotic and exquisite objets d'art known to the world. Using a greater variety of precious and semi-precious stones than any other jeweller, he conjured up rare pieces and executed them with unsurpassed technical skill.

He is noted for his jewelled imperial Easter eggs, which were presented by the tsars Alexander III and Nicholas II to their tsarinas each Easter. The first of these was made in 1884 and was followed by some fifty others, the last in 1917, each with a different theme and most of them miracles of precision work and mechanical novelties. His jewellery employed the most refined enamelled work and gold in a range of different shades, textures and finishes which gave varying effects according to the light or angle of vision.

Fabergé, the son of a St Petersburg jeweller, left Russia to study in London, Paris, Dresden and Frankfurt before taking over the family business at the age of 24. He was joined by his younger brother Agathon, a fine sculptor and painter, and later by his two sons Eugene and Alexander. Around 1900, with branches in Moscow, Odessa, Kiev and London, his staff numbered 500; but the firm ceased after the 1917 revolution.

Exquisite jewelled trinkets by Fabergé. His famous Easter eggs were made for the Russian imperial court

In his jewellery, Fabergé was inspired by the Italian Renaissance, the rococo, and Byzantine and Baroque styles, using sapphires, emeralds and rubies mainly en cabochon, though his diamonds were invariably rose cut in the older style.

Fastenings

Considerable ingenuity has gone into the design of fastenings for necklets and bracelets. Functionally they must be safe in holding two parts together, easy to join and undo, and either unobtrusive or intentionally ornamental.

The snap fastener comprises a small tube into which is pushed a V-shaped spring, with a small protuberance which helps to lock it into position. To open, the spring is compressed with the fingernail and can be easily withdrawn. For broad necklets the snap takes the shape of a box.

The bolt ring applies the principle of a door bolt, with a rounded bar that shoots into a hollowed tube, but for jewellery it is made to form a complete circle, with a coiled spring inside the hollow ring to keep the bar closed.

A simple fastening, with no working parts – the bar and toggle – draws on naval practice. One end of the necklace ends in a short bar, the other with a ring, and when the bar is passed through the ring it sets crosswise to resist any pull.

A terminal used on chains, particularly for suspending watches, is the swivel, which rotates freely on a pivot to avoid twisting the chain. It continues in the form of a spring hoop or loop.

In higher grade necklaces, especially of pearls or precious

Fastenings

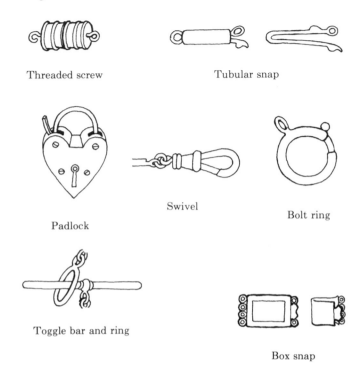

Threaded screw   Tubular snap

Padlock   Swivel   Bolt ring

Toggle bar and ring

Box snap

stones, the fastening is more ornamental, often set with pearls or similar gems to the necklace, enamelled, or studded with marcasites. The snap is set below out of sight. Many clasps in platinum or gold are beautifully made miniature brooches in their own right.

For strength and security in heavier bead and other necklets a barrel snap is used, in which the junction is formed from two circular halves threaded to screw together.

A jump ring is a circular ring – with an opening or slot, enabling it to be attached to other loops or rings as a link, afterwards being either pressed or soldered to close the gap.

Feldspar
There are many varieties in this family of minerals, although for jewellery only two are of any importance – moonstone and labradorite (referred to under those headings). However, since

several feldspars possess unusual specks or streaks of colour, they sometimes find their place in mosaic work or as inlays among agates and other stones. They include a whitish green type known as amazonite, and another displaying flecks of gold or brown, variously known as sunstone or aventurine feldspar.

Fermail
A general title for all kinds of clasps and fastenings, the manufacture of which was an important small industry in the Middle Ages. Those engaged in it, known as fermaillers, had their own corporation in Paris.

Ferronière
A small jewel hanging by a narrow ribbon and so arranged that the ornament comes in the middle of the forehead. It takes its title from the picture in the Louvre of 'La Belle Ferronière' (The Blacksmith's Wife). First worn in Renaissance times it enjoyed a revival in the early part of the nineteenth century, when a small locket was worn in this manner on a narrow black velvet ribbon or fine chain. In early Victorian days a similar arrangement worn around the neck as a choker came into favour.

Fibula
The term generally used in archaeological books for primitive brooches, mainly of the early safety-pin type.

Findings
In all forms of jewellery, a large number of small components are required to make them functional for wearing. These embrace such items as brooch pins, catches and joints; bolt and jump rings; ear ring screws and wires; safety chains, cuff link connections and necklace snaps.

They are known under the generic name of 'Jewellers' Findings'. Since they involve small, intricate work of little artistic merit, they are machine made, mass produced and commercially available in gold, silver and base metals. Although virtually universal, there are some variations in the types and designs manufactured in different countries. However, many artist craftsmen, anxious to offer a wholly hand-made article, make their own such accessories, which they tend to describe as 'fittings', as distinct from the mass produced 'findings'.

Foiled Stones

The aim of all settings is to show off the colour or brilliance of the gem. However, artifice is sometimes used to improve the colour of a pale stone by giving it a backing. The stone, mounted in a closed setting, has a suitably coloured piece of paper or metal foil placed behind it to enrich its appearance and depth of colour. At one time it was common practice to 'foil' a pale blue sapphire by backing it with a blue section of a peacock's feather. Sometimes a clear stone, such as crystal, can be made to simulate a topaz or a garnet by a foil of appropriate colour placed behind it.

It is the general trade practice to make clear to the customer that it is done to enhance the colour of the stone, and not to deceive. Where a necklace consists of a row of the same gems it is important that they should all be of a near match in colour, and skilful foiling can be used to even out variations of shade.

Garnet

The rich, dark red stone which is associated with the name is generally the pyrope or Bohemian garnet. Particularly in the nineteenth century, large and very dark garnets were often en cabochon – uncut with a domed surface – and, to lighten the colour, the underside was hollowed out. The old fashioned name for such stones was 'carbuncles' (glowing coals). Later they were cut in the 'rose' style of diamonds, and used in clusters for brooches and bracelets or set as borders with pearls and other stones. Because of some similarity to rubies, and being mined in South Africa, garnets are sometimes incorrectly sold as 'Cape rubies' or under other names aimed to mislead.

There are two other attractive varieties of this stone – the violet red known as almandine, found in India, Sri Lanka, Brazil and many other countries; and a green variety more correctly described as a demantoid garnet.

Giardinetti Rings

Among the most charming of the rings of the seventeenth and eighteenth centuries, the basic design of Giardinetti rings was of flowers in gold and coloured stones – a spray or posy, or a basket of flowers – always worked with great delicacy. The back of the bezel was generally finely engraved in a design corresponding to the theme of the front. The attention to detail and finish is characteristic of the period and style.

Gilding

The process of applying a finish of gold on to base metal or silver is called gilding. For several centuries the traditional technique of fine gilding was employed. This involved coating the surface with an amalgam of mercury and gold; when heated the mercury was driven off as fumes, leaving a fine film of gold which could be brightly burnished. The method was employed for ecclesiastical jewellery and drinking vessels, but is rarely used today except to regild some small worn area.

The discovery of electro-deposition made it possible to deposit the thinnest possible coating quickly and cheaply, in a process similar to electro silver-plating. Hundreds of small jewellery items can be gold plated simultaneously in one tank. The nearer the base metal is to gold in colour, the thinner need be the deposit. The process, developed about 1840, heralded the mass production of inexpensive 'gold' jewellery. Although the deposit of gold is extremely thin, being measured in tenths of a thousandth of an inch, it stands up to reasonable wear and never peels off, though it will wear thin in parts subject to friction. The surface is smooth and even.

Gimmal Rings

Worn as betrothal rings, forms were known in the sixteenth century, but they were also made very much earlier as is evident from the discovery of such rings in the ruins of Pompeii. Gimmals are two rings so constructed that they form a perfect ring when worn together. The name derives from the Latin 'twin'. Sometimes a half was worn by each of two betrothed persons, and both worn by the wife after marriage. Other examples are intertwined and cannot be separated.

An attractive form is that in which a hand is modelled on each half and, when the two parts are worn together, the two hands appear clasped, expressing the hand-in-hand devotion of the engaged couple.

Girandole

An ear ring or a brooch which has three or more drops suspended from a larger stone or framework, the central drop hanging lower to form a V-shape. This triple pendant derives from baroque styles of the eighteenth century, where the drops were often pearls.

Glass
See Paste

Gold is the most adaptable and easily worked of the precious metals. This modern 14-carat gold necklace with textured 'leaves' was designed in Finland

Gold

Gold was one of the first metals discovered by man. It has an unequalled stability and beauty, is indestructible, does not tarnish, resists almost all known acids and other corrosive materials and can be easily worked. Gold is so ductile and malleable that it can be rolled into almost transparently thin leaves and it is possible to draw it into wire finer than hair – an ounce of gold can be spun into a thread fifty miles long. It can be chased and engraved, and alloyed with other metals to vary its colour and hardness.

In England the first charter granted to goldsmiths dates from the reign of Edward III (1327–77). Since then the State has laid down rigid standards governing the production, sale and purity of articles of gold. These regulations are necessary because gold in its pure state is too soft to use on its own, and some control is essential to determine the proportion of other metals used to make a workable alloy. The quality of gold is described in terms of 'carats'

– fine or pure gold being taken as 24. Thus 18-carat gold means that there are six parts of alloy (some other metal) to eighteen part's of gold. The legally established standards for gold in Britain are 22, 18, 14 and 9 carats. All gold articles have to be stamped at an assay office, which tests their quality and then indelibly marks them with standard impressions defining gold content. Anyone who sells, exposes for sale, or exports gold without these hallmarks (so called because the work of assaying and stamping is done by assay offices under the aegis of the Goldsmiths Hall) is liable to a penalty.

The other metals used to dilute gold are mainly silver and copper, depending on the working qualities required. If the finished article involves bending or shaping, mostly silver is used; or more copper or other metals if hardness is required in items such as bracelet snaps or tie pins. The admixture affects the colour, which accounts for some gold being reddish or yellow, or even white.

Many second-hand articles, particularly from the Victorian era, carry a 15-carat mark, which was legal until 1932 when it was discontinued and replaced by the 14-carat standard bringing British practice into line with that of the Continent and America.

Gold coinage – sovereigns and half sovereigns – are of 22 carats, that is twenty-two parts out of twenty-four of fine gold, as are the majority of wedding rings. (*See also* Hall-marks; Wedding Ring)

Granulation

When the tombs of the Pharaohs revealed their secrets, the world was astonished by the splendour of some of the jewellery. Particularly admired was the technical perfection of the filigree and granulation work undertaken at a time when tools and equipment were primitive and soldering processes unknown.

Granulation consists of tiny beads of gold, used to create borders and surrounds or patterns, sometimes with each tiny ball touching its neighbour. The beads on the Egyptian treasures were not formed by moulds or made by any known mechanical process; the early craftsmen took advantage of a natural law which causes all small portions of liquid to assume a spherical form. They poured molten gold from a height into water so that it solidified into rounded granules, in a manner similar to that of making lead shot. These tiny globules were often combined with larger sized beads, made by beating out tiny half-spheres from very thin sheets and then joining the two halves, using clay as a core to provide solidity.

41

Guard Chain
See Chain

Gypsy Ring
In this type of ring diamonds or other precious stones are set embedded into the metal, almost flush with the surface. Radiating lines engraved round the stone give a starlike appearance and an illusion of greater size. Sometimes a gypsy ring is set with three diamonds, all recessed into the gold backing. The style is also known as 'star setting'.

In gypsy rings the stones are recessed into the metal, and often surrounded by engraved 'star' lines to give the illusion of greater size

Hair Jewellery
Human hair would appear to be the least likely material for use in jewellery, but it has an ancient lineage. The origins of the practice lie in the late medieval custom of distributing mourning rings. These were often fine miniature paintings depicting macabre symbols of death's triumph over life and love. In the eighteenth century fragments of a loved one's hair were incorporated into the designs, sometimes as a woven background, or as a tiny lock or curl in the back of a brooch. Occasionally it would lie within a locket or in the hinged lid of the bezel of a black enamelled ring.

The fashion reached a zenith in Victorian times, an age of extreme sentimental fancy, particularly after the death of Prince Albert in 1861 when strict mourning was observed by the Queen and the Court. While most items of hair jewellery were made by professionals, young ladies of the day were able to obtain kits and instruction books to guide them in the art of weaving hair into tiny plaits and basket patterns.

The use of hair in jewellery was not confined to special mourning jewellery. Lockets were worn containing a tiny curl or tress of a child. Rings, bracelets and long chains were made from woven locks, attractively finished with chased gold buckles set with a turquoise or garnet. In particular, the lightness of the material lent itself to long pendant ear rings, usually of one large circle freely swinging within a larger outer one. At one time, also, there was a fashion for elephant-hair jewellery which purportedly brought good luck to the wearer.

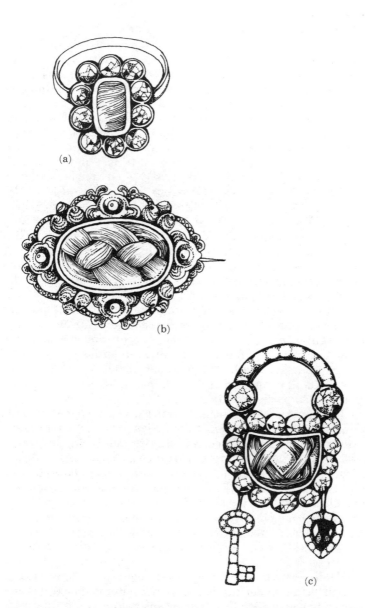

Hair jewellery reached the height of its fashion in Victorian times. (a) Ring
with garnet surround. (b) Filigree brooch with plaited hair. (c) Ornate
diamond and ruby padlock with a central compartment for woven hair

43

Hall-marks

One of the first known forms of consumer protection is that which aimed at guaranteeing the standard of purity of gold and silver articles sold to the public. These costly materials require an addition of some base metal to render them suitable for fabricating, and if no standards existed undue dilutions would be possible, and fraudulent practices made easy.

For some six centuries, royal ordinances and Acts of Parliament have existed, strictly controlling qualities through legal standards. A system was established of impressing a stamp into the metal of the finished article. The powers to test and mark both gold and silver in this manner were vested in the Guild of Goldsmiths. The process was carried out at the Goldsmiths Hall in London (later at other assay offices) and became known as hall-marking. The assay offices are incorporated by royal charter or by statute and are independent of any trade organisation. They certify that the metal used conforms to one of the legal standards of purity or fineness. Testing is carried out from tiny scrapings taken from the articles before they have been finally polished.

The legal standards laid down are:

Gold   9, 14, 18 and 22 carat, indicating the proportion of fine gold in each grade out of 24 parts. Before 1932 recognition was also given to 8 and 15 carat, but both of these were dropped in favour of 14 carat to conform to most European standards.

Silver   Sterling standard: 925 parts per 1,000.

Britannia standard: 958 parts per 1,000.

Platinum   950 parts per 1,000.

The hall-marks feature other stamps which provide valuable information as to the maker of the article, the particular assay office at which it was stamped, and a letter indicating the year of stamping. Since hall-marking was first instituted in the fourteenth century, the designs and individual marks have changed from time to time and new marks have been added. A complete list is invaluable to those seeking to identify antique silver and gold; it is too extensive to include here, there are however many reference works available. A free booklet is available from any of the four assay offices in Britain, and most libraries also provide books on the subject.

The Hall-marking Act 1973 (which came into operation in 1975) made a number of important changes. For instance, it is now an offence to sell or describe an article as gold, silver or platinum (with a few special exceptions) unless it has been hall-marked. It also reduced the number of assay offices in Britain to four –

A complete hall-mark, showing the manufacturer's mark, the mark for sterling silver, the mark of the London assay office and the date mark (in this example for 1976)

Standard marks for British articles

Prior to 1975	Standard	From 1975
	22-carat gold	
	Marked in England	
	Marked in Scotland	
	18-carat gold	
	Marked in England	
	Marked in Scotland	
	14-carat gold	
	9-carat gold	
	Sterling silver	
	Marked in England	
	Marked in Scotland	
	Britannia silver	
—	Platinum	

Assay office marks for British articles

Prior to 1975	Assay office	From 1975
Gold and sterling silver	London	Gold, silver and platinum
Britannia silver		
Gold	Birmingham	Gold and platinum
Silver		Silver
Gold	Sheffield	Gold and silver
Silver		
Gold and silver	Edinburgh	Gold and silver

Former marks of provincial assay offices

Chester

Glasgow

Dublin

Newcastle

Exeter

46

London, Birmingham, Sheffield and Edinburgh – from the many which previously existed.

In many countries the only marks used on precious metals are those struck by the manufacturers. They do not have the kind of legal force and independent certification afforded by British hall-marks.

Identification of Stones
It is almost impossible for a layman to identify a genuine precious stone merely by its appearance. An experienced gemmologist can usually do so by studying it through a powerful lens or a microscope, but even he has to call in the aid of much more sophisticated methods of identification. This is especially so with unusual gems, and synthetic or reconstituted ones. The instruments mainly employed are the refractometer and the spectroscope. These devices determine the behaviour of light through a stone. Every gem has its own individual refractive index. Another check is on the density of the gem (its specific gravity) which is the ratio of its weight to an equal volume of water. One of the most positive means of establishing the exact properties of a stone is the use of X-ray crystallography.

Imitation Stones
The majority of imitation gems are made from glass, using crown glass (window or bottle type) or flint glass. The latter, which contains lead, has a higher refractive index. Practically all imitation stones are soft and can be scratched with a file, and if held to the lips are warm, while genuine stones feel cold. Because of their softness they lose their polish if rubbed by wear. Imitations attempt to copy the precious transparent gems such as diamonds, rubies or emeralds; there is little temptation to reproduce opaque types since their value is so much less.

In recent years many glass-like plastics, particularly the methacrylate and amine plastics, have provided a clear or coloured material which is not only easily mouldable, but produces sharper facets than glass. They are used in some costume jewellery, but their lack of brilliance, light weight and softness precludes them from being mistaken for the genuine gem. (*See also* Paste; Synthetic Gems)

47

Intaglio

Intaglios are the reverse of cameos – the design is incised into the metal or stone instead of standing out in relief. They are widely used for seals which, when impressed on wax, leave a raised image.

In earlier days, especially in the fifteenth and sixteenth centuries, every nobleman carried a signet ring bearing his symbol or crest, and since these symbols were always carved on hard stones like jasper, sardonyx, cornelian and amethyst they have survived to enrich museums throughout the world. The Greeks and later the Romans, with superb sculpturing talent, carved mythological and religious emblems in great detail on tiny stones. In ancient times, all the work was done by the same artist craftsman, from shaping and polishing the stone to the engraving.

Iridium

Iridium is one of six metals closely allied in nature and properties to platinum. It is exceedingly hard and its main use is as an alloy, mainly with platinum, where toughness is specially required. The construction of clips calls for a hard unbending material, and iridium is also used for wire-like divisions between stones which require a knife-edge finish to make them almost invisible when viewed from the front. (*See also* Palladium; Rhodium)

Iron

Iron would appear to have no place in any review of jewellery, but some very fine cast-iron jewellery was the speciality of the Prussian Royal Iron Foundry in Berlin, and it came into vogue as a result of the Prussian war of liberation against Napoleon in 1813. In order to raise funds for arms, patriotic Prussian women gave up their gold jewellery, including wedding rings, and received in exchange reproductions of their gifts, inscribed or with a certificate stating 'Gold gab ich für Eisen' – 'I gave gold for iron'.

Iron jewellery became very fashionable for a decade after the war ended. It was carried out in exquisitely fine filigree work, and

A finely cast bracelet of Berlin ironwork. Such jewellery enjoyed brief vogue in Prussia in the early nineteenth century when gold was scarce

much of it was exported to England and other countries. Unhappily its brittle nature resulted in much of it being broken, and its low intrinsic value meant that it was not treasured and preserved, so that little remains of the large quantities produced. Today pieces of 'Berlin ironwork' are collectors' items.

Ivory
No doubt the fashion for ivory as jewellery originated in the jungles of Africa and India, when pieces of tusk were both a form of currency and objects for wearing. Certainly those that were strung round the neck were the forebears of the popular plain or carved ivory bead necklaces. Skilled carving and more artistic designs brought the material into use for bangles, brooches and charms. Ivory vied with shell for cameos, or was combined with a background of jet and used as an inlay. Victorian memorial jewellery featured carvings of oak leaves and acorns, crosses and hearts in this natural material.

Its source from elephant and other tusks is seen in the characteristic grain, but the quality of ivory varies greatly. The best, which comes from the African elephant, retains a fine, white appearance and is more costly than the Asian type, which has a yellowish shade. Many other materials are often referred to as ivory, such as the teeth of the sperm whale or of hippopotami and the bones of some animals; there is also the seed of a South American palm, the corozo, grown in Ecuador and Colombia, which has a hard white close-grained nature and is turned into many decorative items, especially beads.

Jade
The finest jade is translucent rather than opaque, and although the term jade is associated with a rich green colour, there are many variations, from a creamy white, through shades of buff and brown, to greys, dark green and almost black. When of the finest deep green, it is polished but left plain. Carving is usually carried out on pieces which may have some slight defect as it enables the flaw or imperfection to be cut away.

Two different minerals are known as jade. Jadeite, the harder product, comes from Burma, and nephrite from China, Siberia and New Zealand. The former provides most of the green jade, but also brown, red and mauve, which is mainly used in jewellery. Nephrite is seen as white jade, often with veins and splashings of green, which is mostly finely carved into figures, bowls and decorative vases. Jade was known in China from 3000 BC. The

A hard, fine-grained mineral, jade polishes well to make attractive jewellery such as this gold mounted pendant and bead necklace

Chinese regarded it as being endowed with mystical properties and used it for ritual ceremonies.

Jasper
A variety of the extensive quartz group of minerals, jasper is an impure, opaque stone found in a wide range of colours including white, yellow, red, green and brown, and usually mottled like marble. A common material, its hardness lends itself to fine intaglio carving, the detail being undiminished through centuries. Rare Roman specimens, embodying portrait heads, mythological subjects and animals have been preserved in fine condition.

Jet
This striking glossy black material is a form of fossilised driftwood found in the shale beaches off the Yorkshire coast, where Whitby became the centre of production in the nineteenth century. When the Court went into mourning for the death of Prince Albert in 1861, Queen Victoria decreed that only black jewellery would be worn, and jet, which had previously only had a limited appeal, became fashionable for brooches, bracelets, ear rings, necklaces and hair ornaments. From a cottage industry producing simple hand-made pieces, the manufacture of jet jewellery developed into an industry which kept many factories in the district occupied, and craftsmen became skilled in chasing, engraving and carving attractive items.

Changes in fashion brought about the decline of a vogue which lasted only for some twenty years. In addition there was competition from French jet (a form of black glass) and new synthetic materials which could be pressed or moulded. There has, however, been a revival of interest in wearing jet from time to time, particularly for evening wear.

Butterfly hair pins
in carved jet

Jewish Rings

These large, ceremonial rings are not worn in the ordinary way, but are generally kept in the synagogue and used only for the wedding ceremony. The bezel takes the form of a small building, believed to represent the Temple or Ark of the Covenant. They have been widely copied, but very few genuine old specimens are available, the finest known examples from the sixteenth and seventeenth centuries are displayed in the British Museum, in London.

A Jewish ceremonial ring. The bezel
represents the Ark of the Covenant

51

Jump Ring
See Fastenings

Keeper Ring
Among the many styles of once popular rings that have fallen into disuse is the keeper ring, the name given to a heavy gold ring with all over engraved or chased patterning. It was worn with the wedding ring as a safeguard against the accidental loss of the latter, and regarded also as a portable form of wealth.

Labradorite
A mineral of the feldspar variety, labradorite at first glance is a drab, rather greyish shade; but owing to its special composite structure, it provides attractive optical effects when seen at different angles. As a piece is moved around brilliant greens, yellows or reds sweep across its surface. Because of this quality it is usually fashioned in flat pieces, mainly suitable for brooches, pendants and occasionally signet rings. It is found in profusion in Labrador, as its name implies, and also in the Ukraine and the Urals.

Lapidary
A craftsman skilled in the art of cutting, polishing or engraving precious stones. Most of such work is in fashioning gems suitable for jewellery from the rough mined stone. However, the lapidary is often required to recut in more modern styles stones that, because of their old fashioned cut, are not as bright as they might be, or to reshape stones from old jewellery for a newly modelled piece. He also carries out repairs such as grinding flat a chip or fissure. (*See also* Cutting)

Lapis Lazuli
A rich, dark blue opaque stone with brassy specks of iron pyrites. Its unusual name is from a medieval Latin word meaning blue, derived from Arabic 'al-lazward' – 'sky'. It passed into French during the Crusades in the form 'azur' which has become the English word of azure today. At one period, until the discovery of ultramarine, ground-up lapis lazuli was used for the blue in artists' colours. Its use in jewellery is mainly confined to beads and rings, particularly men's signet rings.

The lapis lazuli mines in Afghanistan have been worked for about 6,000 years. Other sources are Siberia, Chile, Burma and California. A stone often described as Swiss lapis is in fact dyed jasper.

52

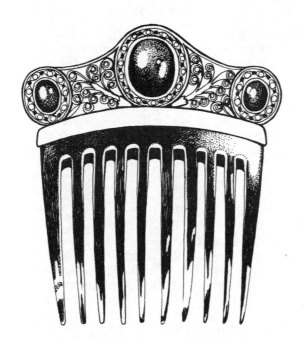

A tortoiseshell comb with gold filigree mount, set with pearls and cabochon cut lapis lazuli. It is part of an eighteenth-century parure

Lockets

Lockets have come and gone with fashion through various periods, but they have always been a popular form of carrying a miniature painting or a photograph. The classical type is the hinged locket with cover, often heart-shaped but with variations in rectangular, square and fancy shapes. Occasionally the front is

Engraved lockets of the late Victorian era

set with a single diamond or other stone, or with chased or engine-turned patterning. A popular version at one time was the locket in the shape of a book, usually hung from one corner. Lockets are hung from chains worn around the neck, or from a brooch.

Somewhat similar are photo pendants, with a picture or lock of hair being visible through a crystal or glass front.

Lost Wax Process
See Cire Perdue

Lustre
See Pearl

Malachite
An ornamental opaque stone in a rich green colour with bands and veining in white and lighter shades of green. The twisting markings no doubt gave rise to its alternative name of serpentine.

Produced in flat slabs, malachite is mostly set in brooches, and was particularly used in Russian nineteenth-century jewellery. Otherwise, it is cabochon cut for rings and decorative beads. It is also inlaid into marble and wood for jewel boxes, work boxes and decorative tables.

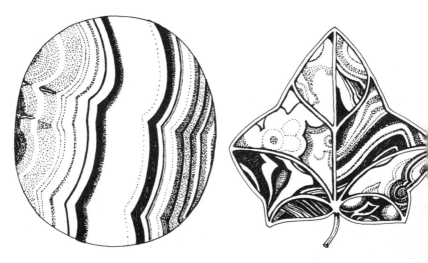

(*Left*) Polished malachite. (*Right*) An ivy-leaf malachite brooch, inlaid with silver wires, dated 1851

Marcasite

Many substitutes have been sought to provide the glittering effect of diamonds. One of the most successful is marcasite, a form of iron pyrites. Although opaque it can be hand-faceted to provide a lively sparkle. It came into fashion under Louis XIV when, set in silver, in floral sprays and rosettes, it was used in brooches and buckles of exceptionally fine workmanship. Some of the finest pieces are set on a background of deep cobalt-blue glass over gold foil, with the marcasite in designs of the most delicate florets and baskets of flowers.

A considerable amount of poorer quality marcasite jewellery was made in later years, but it was much coarser in style, and the tiny stones were drilled into the metal instead of being set.

Marquise Ring

The name marquise is today used to describe any large oval or boat-shaped ring. The original variety came into fashion in the last half of the eighteenth century. It was large – sometimes as long as 38mm (1½in) – and since it filled the space on the finger between the knuckle and first joint it was necessarily worn alone. The shape was generally oval or long octagonal, often coming to a point at the ends, and the finest specimens had a background of rich blue enamel or glass over a ribbed or matted gold background. It was strongly curved to fit the finger.

The centre stone was often a single diamond shaped to accord with the perimeter, or a group of smaller ones; and the bezel had a border of fine small diamonds, invariably set in silver. Sometimes the small stones were studded over the coloured background like stars, or arranged as a posy or basket of flowers. While deep blue was the most popular background, many rings featured puce, yellow, grey or green, and some samples used moss agate as a base instead of glass.

Materna Ring

Some years ago an effort was made to introduce a new type of ring to indicate that a woman had achieved motherhood, and which she could add to her wedding, engagement and possibly eternity ring. The jewellery trade called it the materna ring. It had two loops that between them held a circle to represent the new life created. The symbolism was carried further in a variation which featured a single central gem: a sapphire for a boy and a ruby for a girl. Perhaps not surprisingly, it did not attain any popularity.

The materna ring symbolises the creation of new life

Memorial Jewellery

A distinct class of jewellery worn as a mark of respect for the dead or as a permanent memento of some loved one, mourning and memorial jewellery is a fashion peculiar to England which never appears to have found any popularity in Europe.

Large quantities of rings and brooches of this type were made after the Restoration, in memory of Charles I; and patriotic supporters in succeeding periods wore such mementoes of their monarchs. This jewellery usually incorporated small miniature portraits painted on vellum or ivory. Less famous individuals would be commemorated by their initials and date of death.

Rings would normally be of black enamel with a pearl or diamond. Many later featured a small lock of the deceased's hair in a tiny frame. In the eighteenth century it was common for a man to bequeath a sum of money to be spent on rings to be worn by his friends in his memory. Brooches took a more macabre style.

Mourning brooch in gold, black enamel and onyx, a typical example of the sentimental memorial jewellery that was so much a part of the Victorian era

56

Miniatures and initials were replaced by symbolic devices: skulls, crossbones, tombstones, weeping willows and funeral urns, usually framed in black and inscribed 'In Memoriam'.

When Queen Victoria came to the throne she established rigid codes of mourning which embraced both dress and jewellery, for the Court and the public. The periods of full and half mourning could extend over a period of two years. The death of Prince Albert brought into popular use not only masses of jet jewellery, but black enamel and other variations in rings, brooches, pendants and tie pins. Commemorative jewellery was not always, however, associated with death. It was often exchanged to celebrate romantic attachments, a business partnership or, like 'Mizpah' rings, given for luck; and regimental badges were worn by both men and women as mementoes.

Milanese Chain
The remarkable effect that can be achieved by machine-made jewellery is exemplified by Milanese design chain, which has the appearance and flexibility of knitted fabrics. It is in effect woven metal – usually gold or silver – with very small links interlocking in united courses. The use of gold of more than one colour adds to the impression of woven ribbon. Sometimes small gems are set at intervals on its length. It is much used for watch or other bracelets, and can be adjusted in length by means of a buckle and tongue passing through eyelets. Another attractive usage is for bows from which to hang a watch or brooch, and at one time it was popular for evening bags.

Mohs' Scale
One of the fundamental attributes of a gem is its hardness, and various methods have been practised through the ages to compare the hardness of one stone against another. The simplest was to ascertain which stones would scratch other less hard ones, but the method lacked accuracy. An Austrian mineralogist, Friedrich Mohs (1773–1839), devised a system and established a scale with 10 for the hardest, diamond, 9 for corundum (ruby and sapphire), 8 for topaz, down to the softest of minerals, talc, at 1. Grades 10 and 9 were classified as precious gems.

Thereafter the issue is less clear, because while emerald is graded as $7\frac{1}{2}$ for hardness, it is accepted as precious owing to its rarity and value. Chrysoberyl ($8\frac{1}{2}$), topaz (8) and spinel (8) are generally regarded only as semi-precious, even though of above emerald hardness, because of their greater abundance.

57

Moonstone
One of the large family of minerals known as feldspar. Ranging from virtually colourless to whitish yellow, the moonstone possesses an unusual sheen and the most favoured variety is that which has a beautiful blue bloom. It is invariably cut in cabochon form, and mounted in the minimum of setting so that the light can be reflected through its opal-like milky depths.

Morse
A clasp or brooch used to hold a cape together.

Mosaic
The technique employed in some of the fine pavements in Rome, in which coloured pieces of marble and other stone were inlaid into a pattern, provided the inspiration for mosaic jewellery. Mainly used in brooches, it first became popular in Italy about 1850. Florentine mosaic consists of extremely small pieces of coloured stone inlaid into a stone background, usually black. Venice and Rome produced glass mosaic jewellery, where minute fragments of glass were cemented onto the flat surface of a brooch. The finest work was so delicate that it gave the illusion of a painting.

The style adapted itself to memorial rings and brooches, or to linked mosaic medallions as necklaces. The manufacture of this type of work spread to most of the tourist centres of Italy, and it is probable that in developing this souvenir market the quality of the work was debased, so that only the older and finer examples are prized.

Mother of Pearl
The pearly lining of the shell of the pearl-producing oyster provides a scintillating material which has found many applications. From medieval to modern days craftsmen have carved mother of pearl into beads for necklaces, or for inlays, brooches, crosses and religious emblems. It has been made into collar studs, cufflinks and tie pins, plain or combined with onyx, enamel and gold.

The shells from which the material comes are mainly Australian, some 30cm (12in) to 38cm (15in) wide; but Iranian and Venezuelan shells are sent to European factories for manufacturing. In America, mother of pearl with iridescent colours, known as abelone pearl, finds favour for jewellery.

Necklace, Necklet

The terms necklet and necklace are used as interchangeable descriptions, but they are distinguished by their lengths. The necklet is the shorter ornament, worn close to the neck, usually being 41cm (16in) to 46cm (18in) in length; the necklace may be twice as long, the usual length being anything from 51cm (20in) to 91cm (36in). Another variation is the choker, worn closer to and higher on the neck than the necklet.

Massive gold and silver necklace with a sculptured appearance, the work of a modern Swedish designer

Nephrite
See Jade

Niello
This is enamelling of a sombre kind in which the composition used is mainly lead with some silver and copper, giving a darkish-grey appearance. It lacks the glassy surface of enamel, but has an attractive metallic lustre. Technically, niello is a combination of engraving and enamelling, since the engraver cuts the channels to make the pattern, and the niello material is filled level with the

top. It is specially suited for flat items, or for domed surfaces where the design shows to the best advantage.

Niello is a process known since the Middle Ages. Its main practitioners are the Russians, who have employed it on both silver and gold to decorate rings, brooches and pendants as well as on larger pieces of silverware such as cigar and snuff boxes. Niello is also employed in Tula work – a particular kind of silverwork, sometimes partly gilt, which was first made in Tula, a town in central Russia, in the nineteenth century.

Onyx

This stone is distinguished by its bold light and dark bands. It is a member of the large family of minerals that includes agate and quartz. The black and white contrast is effective in brooches, but onyx is often dyed black to provide a deep velvety appearance as a foil for setting a single pearl or diamond in ear rings or cufflinks.

An onyx cameo brooch in high relief, bordered with pearls

Opal

The opal is unique among gemstones, being neither completely opaque nor transparent. It does not have a crystalline formation as other stones, but is a hardened silica 'jelly' whose prismatic beauty is due to the breaking up of light by its peculiar structure.

Opal owes its milky appearance to myriads of tiny cracks in its surface. Although all types possess this unique rainbow-like play of colours, there are many variations. White opals, from the White Cliffs field in New South Wales, have a cloudy appearance reflecting blue, red and green; while from the same area come black opals, with similar play of colours on a black background. The fire opal is a Mexican variety, of an orange-red hue, only slightly opalescent; and another Mexican type is the water opal, pale and almost colourless, but with an elusive play of other colours. Opals which feature bands or streaks of colour are described as flame opals, while some varieties which show odd patches of colour like mosaics are known as harlequin opals.

Since opals are fragile, and are mined in thin pieces, they are often mounted with some of the rock matrix adhering beneath. And occasionally very thin opals are 'foiled' by having small pieces of coloured silk placed behind them in a closed setting.

The colour variations of opal are infinite, and producing a necklace of carefully matched stones such as this would be a test of skill for any jeweller

Palladium

A natural white metal belonging to the platinum family, palladium is often referred to as white gold since it does not tarnish or change appearance in different atmospheric conditions. It has advantages over platinum in being somewhat cheaper, melting at a lower temperature, and being less dense. An ounce of palladium therefore gives the jeweller a larger volume of metal than an equivalent weight of platinum. For instance the weight of, say, earclips in this metal would be only half that of platinum.

Parure

A French word, used to describe a matched suite of jewellery. A complete set usually comprises necklace, bracelet, ear rings and brooch; but can also embrace a tiara or hair ornament, a buckle and possibly a pair of matching bracelets. A demi-parure is normally two matching items only, such as a necklace and ear rings.

Cut steel parure comprising ear rings, tiara, bracelets and necklace

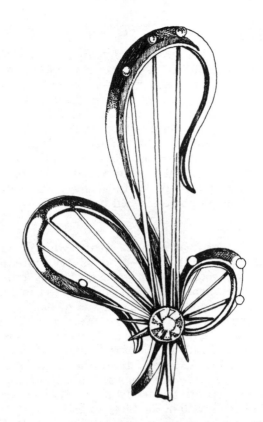

Gilt brooch set with a paste 'diamond'. Good quality paste stones can be hard to distinguish from genuine gems

Paste

Imitations of natural gemstones have existed in all ages. Ancient Egyptian jewellery 'stones' of blue and red glass have been found, and ever since those days glass has formed the majority of imitation gems, either used colourless to simulate diamonds, or in a range of colours created by an admixture of metallic salts. Glass copies of gems are usually known as 'paste' – the name deriving from Italian 'pasta', or dough, because in most cases imitations are cast under pressure in a mould to give them a faceted form before polishing.

Glass with a high proportion of lead is more brilliant and accordingly is the best material to imitate diamonds. To give extra 'fire', such copies, made in Bohemia, have the backs of the stones coated with a mercury amalgam. French types are often backed with a bright metal cap.

63

Strass is a special kind of paste invented by Josef Strasser in Paris about the middle of the eighteenth century, when paste ornaments enjoyed an enormous vogue. Such ornaments were extremely graceful in design, and set with great skill, as a result of which they have become of considerable interest and value. Moreover, antique paste has a softness of colour and mellowness which adds to its charm. Many of these old pieces have been set in silver and pewter. Diamond paste is much more common than coloured stones, as emeralds, rubies and sapphires were less fashionable towards the end of the eighteenth century when making and setting of paste reached its zenith.

Pearl

The name pearl conjures up a subtle, creamy white colour, but the range of shades of pearls is wide – from silvery white to greenish black, soft cream, rose, yellow, grey and bronzy tones. Unlike other prized gems which originate in the earth's surface, pearls are of animal origin and are formed inside the shells of oysters. The pearl-bearing oyster is not the edible variety, but a large type of mussel, producing a pearl known as 'oriental'. There are also freshwater pearls in English mussels found in rivers. They are usually smaller and less lustrous than oriental pearls, although some fine specimens have been found. There is a famous row of fifty-two graduated pearls from Scottish rivers which was worn by Mary Queen of Scots; and in the Victoria and Albert Museum, in London, there is a brooch which has a border of fine Welsh pearls.

The pearl is formed from the deposit of the pearly substance, nacre, by the mollusc. It is believed that a grain of sand or some irritant causes the oyster to coat such a foreign body with its secretions. Thousands of these concentric layers form the pearl, and it is this structure of overlapping platelets that produces the unique sheen and faint iridescence known as the pearl's 'orient'. The length of time it takes for the pearl to grow within its host's shell is governed by the oyster's life span, estimated at eight years.

The value of a pearl is determined by several factors: the perfection of its shape, freedom from dents or blemishes, its size, colour and weight. The finest pearl is the pure round one, white with just a touch of translucency. A chalky look diminishes its value. Then comes the drop or pear shape. Button pearls are domed with a flat underside; they are used mainly in rings, ear rings, tie pins and brooches where the base is partly masked by the setting. Small pearls are usually split in half and used in borders, or in designs with other small gems.

A large baroque pearl set in enamelled gold, with diamonds and rubies. Made in Italy in the sixteenth century, this ornate piece is known as the 'Canning' jewel

Graduated pearls set in a gold collar make a sleek modern piece of jewellery

Very irregularly shaped pearls are known as baroque. They featured much in Renaissance jewellery where clever use was made of their distinctive shape to form figures of birds and animals, often embellished with enamel. They were also used as drops on magnificently decorative pendants. Blister pearls are a pearly formation of irregular shapes found on the inside of the oyster shells. These are often hollow. Seed pearls are real pearls of a size less than quarter-grain.

The value of a well matched row of pearls is considerably in excess of the combined individual value of the separate pearls,

G & J e

since matching in size, colour and shape can involve a lengthy search. It was once a pleasing custom for a man to give his wife or daughter a single pearl each year on her birthday to make a row, using the interim period to seek matched companions. Pearls seem to improve by exposure, and proximity to the skin, and can lose some of their lustre if stored away.

Cultured pearls are produced within the oyster, but the process is speeded up by inserting a glass or mother of pearl bead into the shell, which then acquires the same build-up of secretions as in the natural product. The thickness of the coating of nacre depends on how long the oyster is kept under water in its cage.

Imitation pearls are produced by coating glass beads with a pearly substance obtained from the scales of fish. A cheap pearl gets one coating, a better grade perhaps thirty or forty. Imitation pearls feel smooth when drawn across the teeth, whereas natural or cultured pearls have a gritty or rough feel.

Peridot

This attractive yellowish-green stone has an alternative and more descriptive name of olivine. A somewhat similar coloured stone, the green demantoid garnet, is often incorrectly called peridot. The primary source is St John's Island in the Red Sea, which has produced some large size peridots of a good green colour. A golden-brown variety comes from Arizona.

The peridot had a considerable vogue in early Victorian days, when it was freely used with seed pearls or as a central stone with a surround of other gems.

Peridot brooch showing two cutting styles; emerald cut for the top stone, with a pendeloque drop below

Pinchbeck

The word 'pinchbeck' has in recent years come to imply sham or false, but the material has a true worth. As a rule the name is not used correctly, having become almost a general term for jewellery made from gold substitutes or materials with a gold-like finish. The genuine material is an alloy of copper and zinc, the secret discovery of a London¯ watchmaker, Christopher Pinchbeck (1670–1732). Its appearance was so like gold that some of the best craftsmen of the day used it, first for less important articles and later to make copies of choicer pieces.

Pinchbeck's alloy retained its colour and did not tarnish, like so many other mixtures attempting to reproduce gold, and there is one theory that he used a slight wash of gold on the surface, which remained in the hollows. The rubbed parts, subject to friction, would keep the metal in bright condition. The quality of workmanship and finish was exceptionally fine in many pieces, and some beautiful watches, brooches, châtelaines, buckles and cane handles were made. A considerable number have survived because their intrinsic value was seldom high enough to warrant melting down, like gold or silver, in hard economic times or war conditions.

On the death of Pinchbeck, his son Edward continued to manufacture and trade, but would not sell the material to other manufacturers. Many attempts, particularly in France, were made to reproduce the metal, with some measure of success. The goldsmiths of the day became concerned at this threat to their trade and instituted legal proceedings. The result was legislation which permitted the alloy to be used only for minor items such as shoe buckles or buttons, which did not directly compete with the regular goldsmith's work.

With Edward's death the secret of the correct method of making the alloy was lost, although metal bearing a close resemblance to it continued to be used until well into the nineteenth century. Then electrogilding, which enabled a coating of real gold to be deposited on almost any metal, made pinchbeck superfluous.

Platinum

It is less than two hundred years since platinum was discovered in Russia and later in Colombia, and at first its high price and comparatively short supply limited its use. But when it was discovered in the Transvaal and, much more plentifully, in Canada, around 1930, its use became more common, even though its price has always been beyond that of gold.

Platinum is one of the heaviest of metals. It always remains bright and has a high resistance to chemicals. It provides the perfect setting for diamonds, the whiteness of the metal reflecting into the stones. Platinum is sometimes used to provide an inner band on a plain gold wedding ring to enhance its value; and gold rings can also be enriched by an inlaid floral band of carved platinum.

Until recent legislation, there was no legal obligation to hall-mark platinum, though an international standard of purity was established of 950 parts per 1,000 in most European countries. The custom adopted was to mark such articles with a stamp PLAT. When some parts of, say, a gold ring are of platinum, it will generally be found that they have been marked with the gold quality and added PT – eg 9ct PT, 18ct PT. However, a new hall-marking act which came into operation in 1975 established for the first time a legal hall-mark for platinum.

A spray of diamonds caught in an elegant platinum leaf setting. Platinum's comparative rarity makes it one of the most expensive of the precious metals

Poison Ring

Known from ancient days, any poison rings which have survived are relics of the sixteenth and seventeenth centuries. They were mainly of two kinds. One form had a hinged bezel covering a tiny box in which some potent poison could be carried by those who were in fear of imprisonment or torture. The other had a small projecting pin impregnated with poison, a scratch from which could cause death. The poison could retain its virulence for many years.

There are however many rings with tiny boxes in their bezels, openable by a hinged lid or sliding top, which are described or sold as poison rings but which served no such grim purpose. The boxes were used to house small religious relics, cosmetics, or a lock of hair.

Posy Ring

The giving of rings, from early Roman times to the present, has always been a sign of regard or affection. It is hardly surprising therefore to discover that many such gifts carried written messages, sometimes the lettering being on the outside of the ring, sometimes on the inner surface. There is a belief that the traditional narrow wedding ring is a modern derivative from the old posy ring, which was decorated with flowers and carried an inscription. The word 'posy' however does not relate to the flower decoration, but is taken from 'poesie', as most of the inscriptions were in verse, often French or Latin. The posy ring is also referred to as the motto or chanson ring.

Precious Stones

Although rarity and beauty are factors which affect value, technically the division between precious and semi-precious stones is determined by their hardness based on the Mohs' scale. Diamonds, rubies, emeralds and sapphires are those generally accepted as being precious, and all others semi-precious. However, this demarcation is blurred by the fact that especially fine samples, such as a choice aquamarine, can rank at least equal to if not higher than an indifferent sapphire. There is a current tendency to avoid a strict division between the terms and use the name 'gemstones' to cover the whole range.

All gemstones are of great antiquity, formed in the earth by volcanic explosions, earthquakes and untold pressures long before the advent of mankind. (*See also* Mohs' Scale)

Quartz

Of all species of stones, the most prolific and widely used in jewellery are the members of the quartz family. Their distinctive names, such as bloodstone, onyx, agate, sardonyx, jasper, are designations which were given many centuries ago, according to their colour or markings, before their underlying unity of chemical structure was known. Colour alone is an uncertain guide in classifying such stones, as dyeing is widely employed to obtain different effects; agate, for instance, is hardly ever marketed in an undyed state.

Rhinestone

Real rhinestones are cut from rock crystal. The quality for which they are admired is their characteristic brilliance of colour. At one time a factory on the Rhine, from which their name arises, fashioned the stones from raw crystal imported from the Alps. However, the majority of rhinestones used in modern jewellery are made of a special kind of glass developed to imitate the genuine stone. By fusing a flux of three colours of glass – red, green and blue – a sparkling multi-coloured effect is created.

Rhodium

A metal which, in recent years, has been used to add a brilliant silver-like finish to platinum and diamond jewellery by electroplating. A member of the platinum family of metals, rhodium is both whiter and harder than platinum and, being untarnishable, retains its high finish. It is occasionally used as an alloy with platinum.

Rivière

A necklace of one or two rows of large, evenly matched or graduated gems, often diamonds. Each stone is set in its individual collet and joined by chains to its neighbours. Sometimes rivière necklaces consist of linked garlands of stones, narrowing at the neck and wider and deeper at the front.

Rocaille

This is a term used for types of ornament, mainly brooches and necklaces, based on sea shells, rocks and crustacea.

Rolled Gold

This term describes a process by which a thin sheet of gold is allied to a backing of base metal. The base metal is usually brass or

A rivière of diamonds, c. 1850

gilding metal (90 per cent copper and the rest zinc or other alloy), and when the combined block is subjected to heat and pressure a virtual welding takes place. This is then repeatedly rolled to provide a sheet or ribbon as thin as 1/1,000in. The appropriate piece of jewellery is then manufactured in the normal way as if the metal was all gold. There is never any danger of the two layers splitting part, so complete is the fusion.

As goods made from rolled gold do not require hall-marking, there is no means of knowing the carat standard of the gold layer, nor its thickness. However, the surface at least is real gold, and rolled gold pieces have stood the test of time and given excellent wear.

The *gold filled* process is somewhat similar to rolled gold, except that a second thin layer of gold is fused to the underside of the base metal core, making a three-ply sandwich.

Rondelles
In bead necklaces thin discs of clear crystal, known as rondelles, are sometimes interspersed between the threaded gems. This is done not just to extend the length but is a traditional method of isolating each bead to give it an air of individuality. Occasionally, round plain or engraved glass beads are used as rondelles. They introduce neutrality into a coloured chain and vary the effect.

Rose Cut
A method of cutting gems, mainly diamonds, in which the base is flat and the upper part has a number of triangular facets. (*See also* Cutting)

Rose Quartz
As its name implies, this is the rose-red and pink type of quartz which, although an attractive material, is unsuitable for choice jewellery mainly because its surface is riddled with fine cracks, with a mottled crystalline appearance. But these qualities, allied to its semi-translucent nature and pleasing colour, render it ideal for pendants and beads. More particularly it is a prized material for carvings of figures and animals.

Ruby
There are few gems which can match the gorgeous colour of a fine ruby. It ranges from a clear pale rose to a rich carmine red. This last is the highly esteemed 'Burma' ruby with a deep saturated redness. 'Siamese' rubies tend to have a brownish tinge, somewhat like a garnet. The 'Ceylon' ruby, although paler in colour, is compensated by having more sparkle. These are the three

Matching 'daffodil' ear clip and ring set with rubies. Large-sized rubies are rare but clusters of small stones are both attractive and valuable

principal rubies, the country in each name indicating not only their source, but being a generally recognised term for their colour. At one time, Queensland was a source of supply of another variety, the anakie ruby. Rubies are also found with a star effect and accordingly are known as star, or asteria, rubies.

Very few really large rubies mined are free from flaws. A good sized one in the much admired 'pigeon's blood' colour and without defects is the most expensive of all gems. Consequently, any large red stone offered as a ruby should be looked at critically, particularly as it was common at one time to designate certain colours of garnets as 'Ceylon ruby', 'Arizona ruby', 'Bohemian ruby', 'Colorado ruby' and other names because of their apparent similarity to the genuine gem.

It is difficult to believe that the ruby and sapphire both belong to the corundum family, both having the same nature. It is only slight changes in the metallic oxides within them that creates such strikingly diverse colours.

Sapphire

A very beautiful stone, the sapphire is usually thought of as blue, although there are a number of variations of colour in this gem. The most prized is the velvety blue Kashmir sapphire, although unfortunately only a small percentage of the output of these mines reaches the ideal colour. Some fine blue stones are found in Thailand and Burma. A much lighter colour characterises the 'Ceylon' sapphire, but its paler shade is compensated for by a greater liveliness of appearance. Several districts of Australia yield sapphires, the largest sizes coming from the Queensland fields. Their colour is of so dark a blue, from indigo to an almost blackish green, that some of their beauty is lost in artificial light; but stones of 15 or even 20 carats are not unusual. A fairly recently discovered source in Utah yields the Montana sapphire of a hard, cold appearance.

The white sapphire has a soft, rich lustre, and is frequently used as a substitute for a diamond, while the yellow sapphire is more brilliant than the somewhat similar topaz. There are several shades of green, and an amethyst variety called mauve sapphire; while pink varieties were employed in much Georgian jewellery. Star sapphires, invariably used in rings, are cabochon cut, their three luminous lines crossing to form a shimmering star, and their tint being almost grey.

Although of the same family (corundum) as the ruby, the sapphire is much commoner than its sister stone and is mined in

Sapphire and diamond suite, comprising necklace and ear rings

larger sizes. A great deal of symbolism attaches to this stone. In the Middle Ages it was believed to be of great help to the wearer in leading a good and pure life, and in the thirteenth and fourteenth centuries it was set in rings for priests and bishops.

Sard
This brownish-red stone is of the same nature as the cornelian. Its principal use in jewellery has been as an intaglio for seals.

Sardonyx
A member of the extensive quartz family, this stone is distinguished by its two layers. The reddish-brown layer is the sard, and the second, which has bands of black, grey, white or brown, is typical of onyx configuration. Craftsmen dating back to early Greek and Roman days used the material for exquisite seals and cameos. The carver would take advantage of the colours in the layers to show, say, cream-coloured figures on a dark background, or to depict drapery. Accidental stains or tones in the material were skilfully worked into the design, not only by use of the solid colours, but by thinning down the opaque layers to give a remarkable luminous, transparent effect.

Scarf Pin
See Tie Pin

74

Seals

Some of the finest examples of seals date from Roman times and from a revival of classical art in the eighteenth century. Choosing hard and rare stones, both Greeks and Romans carved subjects from their own mythology in astonishing detail, considering the small compass of a gem. Each stone was carefully selected as a suitable background for the subject: Pluto, god of the Underworld, appeared on a dark stone such as cornelian or jasper; Bacchus, god of wine, on purple amethyst; the sea-goddess Amphitrite on an aquamarine.

Apart from their use in rings, many seals were handsomely mounted in gold and worn round the neck on a chain, or affixed to ivory, marble and wood handles for desk use. No Victorian or Edwardian gentleman would fail to have one hung on his gold Albert watch-chain spread across his waistcoat, or worn as a fob to his watch with evening dress. (*See also* Intaglio; Signet Ring)

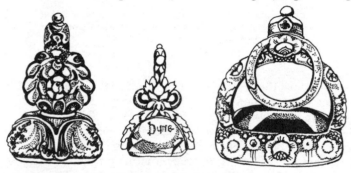

Carved gold fob seals of typical nineteenth-century design

Sévigné

Named after Madame de Sévigné, the French writer of letters, this bow-shaped bodice ornament of gold or silver lavishly set with stones was fashionable in the seventeenth century. The basic form is often elaborated with openwork floral motifs, and sometimes has added drops in the girandole style.

Signet Ring

The signet is one of the earliest types of ring, at one period worn only by persons of standing since the right to wear such an ornament was restricted to certain citizens and officers. It was often used as a symbol of authority or authenticity in the fifteenth and sixteenth centuries; before handing over valuables to a messenger a banker might demand to see his ring. Consequently, it was the custom for the plain gold bezel to be engraved with the arms, initials or symbol of the owner; in fact the table, as the flat top is called, was often in the shape of a shield to carry the coat of arms or crest. Many were set with intaglio seals used to impress on wax in place of a signet.

Modern signets often have square, oval or fancy-shaped bezels, plain or with engine-turned designs on them, and sometimes a single diamond is inset. Combinations of platinum and gold, and carved, engraved or stepped shoulders, are other variations.

Men's signet rings. Signets are now worn purely for fashion but they were originally used as a means of identification and carried a carved seal. The earliest examples date back to ancient Egyptian times

Silver
Silver provides the craftsman with a material ideally suited both for domestic products and for jewellery. It lends itself to fabrication because of its softness, low melting point, great malleability and capacity for taking a high polish. It is resistant to most acids. Only gold surpasses it in some of these characteristics, but its lower price and greater availability make it not only a natural choice for jewellery, but a useful testing ground for craft techniques such as engraving, chasing and embossing.

The legal standard for all silver articles is 925 parts per 1,000, known as sterling silver. This applies to jewellery as well as domestic and other articles, but many small silver items and component parts of jewellery are free of the obligation to carry the hall-mark.

Most silver jewellery earlier than the nineteenth century was largely or wholly hand-made. The development of machinery, the growth of factories in Birmingham and Sheffield and a tax concession on silver in 1890, opened the floodgates for a mass of popular, cheap silver jewellery. Chains, pendants, trinkets, sentimental souvenirs and bracelets flooded the market when techniques for pressing or stamping parts were developed. Little hand-made silver jewellery is produced today except by individual artist silversmiths and craftworkers. (*See also* Hall-marks)

Versatile silver lends itself well to varying styles:
(*Above*) Two brooches with traditional themes designed by the Danish sculptor,
Georg Jensen (1866–1935). (*Below*) In contrast, two necklaces and an
armband with the stark lines so characteristic of the new generation of
Scandinavian designers

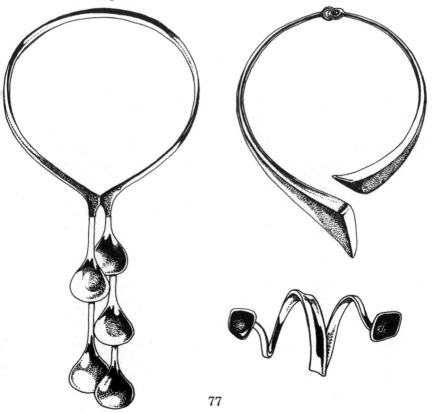

Solitaire
This is a ring with a single stone, usually a diamond.

Spinel
This gem is similar in appearance to the ruby, and its traditional name is balas ruby or ruby spinel. The confusion is compounded because it is found with rubies in the same mines of Burma and the river gravel of Sri Lanka. There is a yellow to orange-red variety known as the rubicelle, and a bright orange coloured specimen known as flame spinel. Many early descriptions of stones as rubies really refer to the spinel. The celebrated Black Prince's ruby and the enormous red stone set in the apex of the crown made for Catherine II of Russia in 1762 are both spinels.

The stone is not found in large sizes but is very suitable for rings, being among the hardest of gems. It is also produced synthetically.

Step Cut
See Cutting

Swivel
See Fastenings

Synthetic Gems
The first steps in making valuable gems by artificial means came in the process of reconstruction, carried out about a hundred years ago. In this process, small particles of real rubies were fused under great heat to form one larger stone. Greater attention, however, has since been devoted to making truly synthetic stones by the Verneuil process, which involves fusing in powder form the chemical constituents of the natural gem.

Although good results have been achieved in creating such artificial stones, the process of bringing the finished product to the state of purity required is both complicated and expensive. Considerable success has been achieved in making sapphires, emeralds, spinels and other stones by the Vernueil process, and it is theoretically possible to produce good sized gems of excellent colour, responding to all the standard tests. With most of them however there is a tendency to brittleness which can cause fractures when being polished and despite this progress there is no synthetic equivalent for every variety of gem.

So long as the description 'synthetic' is attached when such stones are sold, a buyer can accept such gems as akin to the natural product, although without their age or rarity.

Tassie, James

In the eighteenth century, choice gems of many earlier periods were copied in different materials, and among the most beautiful examples were those made in glass by a young Scotsman named James Tassie. Originally a stonemason, hailing from Pollokshaws, near Glasgow, his outstanding skill and artistry were recognised by the award of a bounty in 1765. He made splendid imitations of antique cameos and intaglios, in clear glass in rich colours, with faithful attention to detail. His aim was not to pretend they were old or genuine, but to spread the knowledge of early art, and his products became very fashionable. Made primarily for cabinet collections, many were later mounted in rings, bracelets, brooches and combs. One order, for samples of his whole range, was received from Catherine the Great of Russia.

Although his output was prolific – he is said to have had 15,000 patterns – and sold very cheaply, comparatively few pieces have survived and are collected today for their fine workmanship and finish.

Tiara

This humble bandeau, tied round the forehead to keep the hair tidy, developed over the years into an ornate, regal piece of jewellery. The royal and imperial habit of wearing crowns was paralleled by great ladies of the nineteenth century wearing combs and diadems which developed into the full glory of the diamond-studded tiara. Worn on the forepart of the head in a similar position to the crown, it consisted of ornamental groups rising from the headband, often embodying clusters of scrolls and foliage work, graduated in size.

A tiara, or diadem, designed by May Morris (1862–1938), daughter of the great artist and poet, William Morris

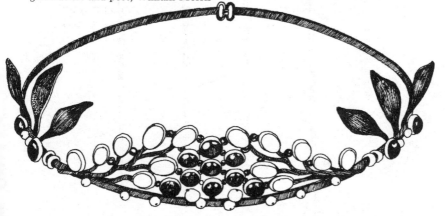

The fashion was at its height in Napoleonic days. Since only dress occasions at Court or the opera provided the opportunity of wearing such expensive and elaborate pieces, jewellers turned their ingenuity to making them serviceable for other purposes, and many tiaras have parts which are detachable and can be assembled on a skeleton frame as a brooch or a pair of clips.

The earlier name for the tiara was the diadem.

Tie Pin

Like most jewellery, particularly that worn by men, the dictates of fashion have determined the rise or fall in popularity of many items. This is particularly true of the scarf and tie pin. In Edwardian days no well dressed gentleman would be without such an ornament in his tie, helping to keep it in place. An enormous range of patterns and designs existed, from a single pearl, diamond or opal, to a cluster of diamonds surrounding a single stone. Popular styles were horseshoes set with gems, sword handles, pheasants, horses, anchors, Masonic emblems, deer and dogs, and almost every kind of sporting badge or emblem. Many were set with gems or carried out in coloured enamels. The range of subjects makes an interesting commentary on contemporary

Late Victorian tie pins. (a) Onyx and gold. (b) Gold and pearl. (c) Gold half-dollar. (d) Gold horseshoe studded with pearls

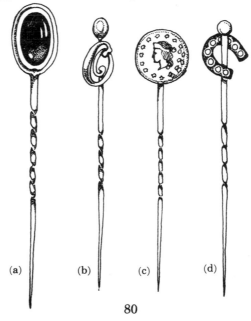

(a)   (b)   (c)   (d)

sports, hobbies and life styles, since many pins were mass produced in cheaper materials to meet the tastes and pockets of all classes of society.

An American introduction was the tie chain, worn usually when coats were left off in summer, the chain falling across the lower part of the tie and held in place by a brooch pin fastened to the shirt. It did not achieve widespread usage in Britain.

Topaz

Although less valuable than most of the precious stones, the golden-yellow topaz is a beautiful gem and one that was extremely popular in the eighteenth and nineteenth centuries. Almost any yellow stone tends to be described as a topaz – incorrectly, since it is really only the fine Brazilian variety which qualifies for the title. Nevertheless, some fine specimens come from Russia. The similarly coloured citrine is frequently referred to as a topaz, but the real confusion arises from a former trade custom of giving special names to a variety of coloured quartz – Madeira topaz, Scotch topaz, Spanish topaz, Occidental topaz, etc.

Colourless topaz is common, and topaz with a blue tinge is

Although one of the lesser gemstones, topaz has been popular in jewellery for centuries. A massive setting such as this necklace shows fine stones to advantage

G & J f

found in the Urals and California. A fine rose-pink stone is usually the result of a special heat treatment of the brownish-yellow variety, carried out on stones regarded as too brown to sell.

The topaz has the characteristic of fading after very long exposure to bright sunlight. It is also inclined to be brittle, and if subjected to a hard knock can sometimes chip or develop an odd feather-like flaw.

Tortoiseshell

Although mineral products are the main sources of raw materials for jewellery, craftsmen of all ages have not been averse to employing any other material that will provide a decorative effect or finish. Among these are animal products such as ivory, bone, coral and tortoiseshell.

The latter has been widely used for combs, buckles, hair slides and watch cases. But for jewellery, in the general sense, it has been used with a special type of inlaid decoration which takes the form of an inlay of tiny gold pins to form patterns, known as 'piqué d'or' or 'piqué work'. In designs of flowers, arabesques and borders, the golden star-like inlays contrast with the polished dark-brown and figured shell. Larger size inlays are described as 'clouté d'or' and 'posé d'or'. The origin of this work is believed to be the beautiful gold and black Oriental lacquer which, throughout the seventeenth and eighteenth centuries, was regarded very highly. Naples was always celebrated for piqué work.

The lightness in weight of tortoiseshell makes it well suited to large ear rings, usually comprising two large loops, the inner one freely suspended within the larger; or in the form of large carved flowers.

Tourmaline

This stone is of special interest to the mineralogist, as it displays the greatest range of colour of any gem. Moreover, many specimens show two or more colours, perhaps red or pink at one end, green at the other, and a colourless area between. Among the main shades are green, red, pink and blue-green; but even in a stone which is predominantly one colour, a variation can be seen according to the side from which it is viewed. This characteristic is known as dichroism. Red tourmaline is generally known as rubellite, and the green or blue-green type as indicolite.

Tourmaline was discovered less than two hundred years ago. The gem-favoured areas of Brazil, Sri Lanka, The Urals, California and Namibia are the main sources.

Troy Weight

The unit of weight for all gold and silver in Britain is the troy ounce. This differs from the common commercial avoirdupois standard. Formerly, the troy ounce was divided into 20 pennyweights (dwt) but is now more generally shown in fractions or percentages of the ounce. One ounce troy is approximately 1.10oz avoirdupois (actually 1.0971). It is 31.10 grams on the metric scale.

The name is said to be derived from the French town of Troyes, where a celebrated fair was held annually; and dates from the reign of Edward III.

Turquoise

One of the earliest stones known, being first mined about 5,000 years ago, the turquoise is a beautiful gem which gives its name to the colour. It was used extensively in jewellery at the end of the eighteenth and during the nineteenth centuries, when it was known as Turkey stone, after the main source at the time. The richest blue specimens are, however, from Iran.

Large-size pieces of turquoise are seldom found without inperfections – small fissures or markings which, while adding character, detract from the value of expensive or finely worked pieces. Accordingly, in much Georgian and Victorian jewellery small stones were set in rosettes and borders, often with pearls.

The stone is, to some extent, porous, and can easily become discoloured by contact with grease or dirty water. Many turquoise stones are artificially stained to improve the colour and appearance, and a high percentage of those sold have been dyed. These tend to turn green with ageing if dyes that are not fast to light have been employed.

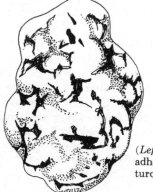

(*Left*) Uncut turquoise with matrix still adhering. (*Above*) Brooch of polished turquoise surrounded by small pearls

Wedding Ring

It was not until the Council of Trent in the sixteenth century that the wedding ring had a recognised place in the marriage ceremony. It was not, at first, the plain gold circlet commonly used in modern times, but often highly decorated.

Because of the special sentiment attached to wedding rings they are invariably bought in the highest possible grade of gold – 22-carat. This was the only recognised standard from 1576 until 1798, when the 18-carat standard was introduced. In 1942, during World War II, a standard 9-carat gold wedding ring was introduced to save gold and the then Board of Trade established a unique distinguishing stamp, consisting of two intersecting circles. Although this special mark was stamped by the assay office, it is not strictly a hall-mark. Such rings had to be completely plain and were limited to a weight of not more than 4dwt (pennyweights). Platinum has become a modern choice for wedding rings, usually with added workmanship by means of faceting, engraving or chasing.

Modern gold wedding rings. The second from the right interlocks with a matching engagement ring

Wedgwood

No reference to jewellery would be complete without a mention of the jasper cameos produced by the Wedgwood factory for use in rings, ear rings, bracelets, pendants and brooches. Unlike true cameos, these dainty productions involve no hand cutting, but are produced by a moulding process, usually depicting heads or figures in white relief on a matt blue, green or black ground. Mounted in gold and silver, they have added a new dimension to jewellery design, and have continued in popularity ever since they were first made in the eighteenth century.

Zircon

Of all natural gems, the zircon is nearest in brilliance to the diamond owing to its high dispersion of light and great refractivity. Because of this, it has often passed under the description of 'Ceylon diamond', and the deception is heightened by the fact that the clear or white variety is cut as a 'brilliant' like a diamond. Various other names have been used throughout the ages for zircons of different colours. Pale and yellow zircons were known as jargoons, the brown variety as zirconites and the reddish-brown stone as hyacinths. The Biblical and medieval stone recorded as the jacinth is assumed also to have been the zircon.

Bluish green zircon has a dazzling colour that is unique among precious stones and is the most popular for rings. Although far from rare – it is found in rock formations in many parts of the world – stones suitable for jewellery are almost exclusively found in Sri Lanka, which has produced zircons of practically every tint that this gem is capable of assuming.

Appendix

A summary of all principal gems, giving their hardness factors, colourings and major sources of supply, follows on pages 86 to 93.

GEMSTONE	VARIETY	HARDNESS	COLOUR	MAIN SOURCES
BERYL	Emerald	$7\frac{1}{2}$–8	Light to dark green	Brazil; Colombia; Egypt; Elba; India; Malagasy Republic; Transvaal; USA (California); USSR (Siberia; Urals)
	Aquamarine		Transparent, pale blue, greenish blue	Brazil; Malagasy Republic; Urals
	Beryl		Green, golden yellow (Helidor), pink/rose (Morganite)	As for emerald
CHRYSOBERYL		$8\frac{1}{2}$	Pale yellow, pale green, opaque and transparent	Brazil; Malagasy Republic; Sri Lanka; USA
	Cat's Eye		Honey coloured, greenish or brownish, showing a streak of light	Brazil; Malagasy Republic; Sri Lanka; USA
	Alexandrite		Greenish in daylight; red to reddish brown by artificial (yellow) light	Sri Lanka; Tasmania; USSR; Zimbabwe

GEMSTONE	VARIETY	HARDNESS	COLOUR	MAIN SOURCES
CORUNDUM	Ruby Star Ruby (Asteria)	9	Various shades of red Star effect	Burma; Sri Lanka; Thailand
	Sapphire		Blue, pale blue, pink, yellow, mauve	Australia; Burma; Kashmir; Malagasy Republic; Sri Lanka; Thailand; USSR (Urals)
	Star Sapphire		Blue, grey with 6-point star effect	As above
	Cat's Eye Sapphire		Blue with shimmering effect	As above
DIAMOND		10	Transparent, blue-white, yellowish, pink, green, mauve	Australia; Borneo; Brazil; Guinea; India; Sierra Leone; South Africa; Tanzania; Zimbabwe
FELDSPAR	Moonstone	6	Colourless, whitish with bluish wavy lines of light	Australia; Brazil; Sri Lanka; USA
	Orthoclase		Gold yellow, lemon	Malagasy Republic
	Labradorite		Opaque, grey background flecks of colour	Canada; Finland; Labrador; Sweden; USA; USSR

GEMSTONE	VARIETY	HARDNESS	COLOUR	MAIN SOURCES
GARNET	Almandine	$7\frac{1}{4}$	Violet-red	Australia; Austria; Brazil; Czechoslovakia (Bohemia); Hungary; India; Norway; Spain; Switzerland; Uruguay; USA; USSR
	Pyrope		Fiery and browny-red	Mostly as for almandine and also South Africa
	Demantoid		Green, yellowish/olive green	USSR (Siberia; Urals)
JADE or JADEITE		$6\frac{1}{2}$–7	Opaque or translucent, white or greyish tending to pink or blue with specks of green	Burma; China; Mexico; Tibet; Turkestan
	Nephrite		Green, white, single colour or flecked, brown and reddish	Alaska; Brazil; China; New Zealand; Peru; Switzerland; Turkestan; USSR (Siberia); Venezuela

GEMSTONE	VARIETY	HARDNESS	COLOUR	MAIN SOURCES
JET		3–4	Opaque; black, dark brown	Britain (Whitby, Yorkshire); E. Germany (Saxony); France; Spain; USA (Colorado); USSR
LAPIS LAZULI		5½–6	Opaque blue often with brassy specks	Afghanistan; South America (Andes); USSR (Siberia)
MALACHITE		3½–4	Emerald to dark green mottled with dark and light bands	Australia; Chile; France; Rumania; USA; USSR (Urals); Zimbabwe
OLIVINE	Peridot	6½–7	Greenish gold, olive-green	Australia; Brazil; Burma; Egypt; Norway; Sri Lanka; USA (Arizona; New Mexico); Zaire
OPAL		5–6	Milky white with shimmering rainbow-like play of colours	Australia; Czechoslovakia; Guatemala; Honduras; Japan; Mexico: USA
	Fire Opal		Reddish yellow, orange, red and green streaks, rarely iridescent	Australia; Mexico; USA (Nevada)

GEMSTONE	VARIETY	HARDNESS	COLOUR	MAIN SOURCES
OPAL (continued)	Water Opal	5-6	Transparent, straw, pale shades	Mexico
	Black Opal		Vivid play of colours on black or dark ground	Australia (New South Wales)
QUARTZ	Rock Crystal	7	Transparent	Brazil; Italy; Japan; Malagasy Republic; Scotland; Silesia; Tyrol; USSR (Urals)
	Amethyst		Transparent, violet shades	Australia; Brazil; France; Hungary; Italy; Malagasy Republic; Mexico; Spain; Sri Lanka; Uruguay; USSR
	Rose Quartz		Milky rose-pink, semi-transparent	Brazil; E. Germany (Bohemia); Ireland; Italy; Japan; Scotland; South Africa; Sri Lanka; USSR; W. Germany (Bavaria)
	Cat's Eye		Greyish green, yellow or blue with streak	South Africa; and several countries as for rose quartz

GEMSTONE	VARIETY	HARDNESS	COLOUR	MAIN SOURCES
QUARTZ (continued)	Falcon's Eye	7	Greyish blue with greenish streak	As for cat's eye
	Chalcedony		Milky, whitish, bluish grey and green-yellow	Brazil; Iceland; Italy; Uruguay
	Blue Chalcedony		Light blue and blue opaque	India; Rumania; USA (Arizona); USSR (Siberia)
	Cornelian		Various shades of red to yellow-brown	Brazil; Germany; India; Japan; USSR (Siberia)
	Chrysoprase		Apple green, light green, with white and grey streaks	Austria; Canada; India; USA; USSR (Urals)
	Jasper		White, yellow, red, green, brown	Brazil; E. Germany (Saxony); Egypt; Italy; South Africa; USA; USSR (Siberia)
	Agate		White, yellow, grey, red, brown, black, stratified, flecked	Asia Minor; Brazil; China; Germany; India; Malagasy Republic

GEMSTONE	VARIETY	HARDNESS	COLOUR	MAIN SOURCES
QUARTZ (continued)	Moss Agate	7	Milky with green or rust coloured inclusions	As for agate
	Onyx		Black and white bands	As for agate
	Aventurine		Opaque. Red-brown and green, spangled with mica	Australia; Brazil; Egypt; France; India; Scotland; Spain; Syria; USSR; W. Germany (Bavaria)
	Sard		Orange, black-brown, brown, semi-transparent	Brazil; Germany; India; Japan; USSR
SPINEL		8	Red, orange, purple, violet, blue, green, dark blue (Ceylonite)	Brazil; Burma; Malagasy Republic; Sri Lanka; Thailand
TOPAZ		8	Translucent, gold, yellow, pink, blue	Australia; Brazil; Japan; Mexico; Sri Lanka; USA (California); USSR (Siberia; Urals)

GEMSTONE	VARIETY	HARDNESS	COLOUR	MAIN SOURCES
TOURMALINE		$7\frac{1}{2}$	Colourless, all colours	Brazil; Kashmir; Malagasy Republic; South Africa; USA (California; Colorado); USSR (Urals)
	Rubellite		Pink, ruby red	Brazil; China; Sri Lanka; USSR
	Indicolite		Greenish shades	As for rubellite
	Yellow tourmaline			Malagasy Republic; Sri Lanka
TURQUOISE		5–6	Opaque, apple green, green, sky blue	Iran; Sinai Peninsula; Tibet; Turkestan
ZIRCON		$7\frac{1}{2}$	Colourless, blue-green, yellow	Australia; Canada; Malagasy Republic; Norway; Sri Lanka; Sweden; Thailand
	Jacinth		Orange-red, red, violet	As above and Brazil; South Africa
	Hyacinth		Reddish-brown	Thailand

INDEX

95